easy stitching

with buttons, beads and braids

C&T PUBLISHING

First Edition published in 2008 by C&T Publishing
P.O. Box 1456, Lafayette, CA 94549
ISBN-13: 978-1-57120-591-9
ISBN-10: 1-57120-591-8

Editor Anna Scott | *Editorial Assistants* Marian Carpenter, Ali Carpenter
Graphic Designer Lynton Grandison | *Pattern Designer* Jennifer Victorsen | *Illustrator* Kathleen Barac | *Stylist* Sue Stubbs
Photographers Sue Stubbs, Seb Szocinski | *Publisher* Margie Bauer

EASY STITCHING WITH BUTTONS, BEADS AND BRAIDS
COPYRIGHT © 2008 COUNTRY BUMPKIN PUBLICATIONS

315 Unley Road, Malvern, South Australia 5061 www.countrybumpkin.com.au

Printed in China

contents

welcome

Beads, buttons, ribbons and braids are
wonderful for decorating your wardrobe,
personalising your home and making fabulous
gifts for family and friends.

Just a few hours and a small collection of
shimmering beads, attractive buttons or colourful
ribbons and braids are all you need to transform
everyday items into truly individual creations.
Fabulous and imaginative bags, a stylish evening
shawl and sensational shirts, a trendy cushion,
chic table linen, the cutest baby booties and a
tutu fit for a fairy princess - can all be easily
made following a few simple steps.

Alternative styles and colour options are
suggested throughout but limited only by your
imagination.

The possibilities are endless and I hope this book
will help you begin a wonderful journey on the
pleasures of embellishment.

Anna

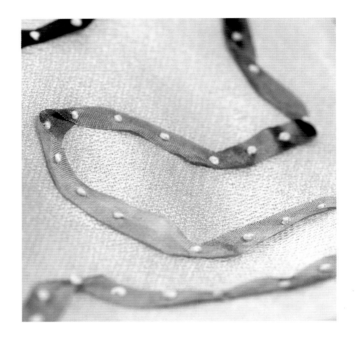

materials

choosing fabrics

Most fabrics, from fine silk and cotton to cosy wool blanketing, furnishing fabrics and felt can be embellished with embroidery.

The kind of project you choose will influence the type of fabric you use. Likewise the fabric will affect the appearance of the finished item. It is important to keep in mind that in most cases the fabric will show through the stitches. Fabrics with patterns or woven textures offer background interest that can add extra dimension to your work.

Thicker threads are used on heavier fabrics. Lightweight fabrics are best worked with finer threads but can be stabilised with interfacing if you wish to embroider with thick threads.

How will you know if the fabric is right?

It is always a good idea to work a small sample on a spare piece of fabric to make sure that the fabric, threads and stitches you are about to use will give you the result you are looking for.

Calico is a plain, firm, unbleached cotton fabric, excellent for embroidery. Calico can be dyed or painted to add extra interest.

Cotton fabrics are among the most durable of fabrics. They are available in a large range of colours, patterns and weights, from fine lawn to heavier denim and twill.

Felt is a very versatile non-woven fabric that will not fray when cut. Traditionally made from wool, today many felts are made from synthetic fibres, so you will need to be very careful if pressing these.

Furnishing fabrics offer some fantastic choices of plain colours or self-patterns, such as damask. You can often obtain small pieces that are suitable for embroidery from upholsterers.

Linen is strong and durable. It has a natural lustre and the creamy white or light tan fabrics are easily dyed. Linen is available in a range of weights from fine handkerchief linen to heavy twill.

Silk is a luxurious fibre that can be made into sensuous fabric available in a large variety of colours. It comes in a range of weights and finishes from fine transparent chiffon and organza to textured silk dupion, heavy twill and brocade.

Wool fabrics come in a selection of weights and finishes, from fine flannel, ideal for baby wraps, to thick and cosy blanketing.

Interfacing can be used to stabilise some lightweight fabrics and to give extra body. Woven and non-woven interfacings are available in a range of weights to suit different fabrics. Some are fusible and others need to be sewn in. Choose an interfacing to match the fabric you wish to embroider. Your fabric supplier will advise you.

HINTS

What is the grain of the fabric?
The grain is the direction in which the threads of a fabric lie.

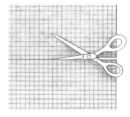

When cutting fabrics, cut along the grain line, following a fabric thread, to ensure you cut straight edges.

What is the bias?

The bias of a fabric runs diagonally across the grain and allows the fabric to 'give' if stretched. If you pull the fabric on the bias you may distort the threads and the shape of a cut piece.

choosing threads

The selection of threads and yarns available for embroidery is extensive.

It is possible to use the very finest of threads right through to lightweight string for stitching. The only real restriction when choosing your thread is that it is suitable for the fabric and type of project you wish to do.

Stranded cottons and perlé cotton threads are some of the easiest and most versatile threads to work with and are also the most readily available.

Stranded cottons are inexpensive, low sheen threads that come in an extensive variety of colours. The threads can be separated into six individual strands and are very easy to work with. You can vary the appearance of your stitches by altering the number of strands – fewer strands create finer stitches.

Perlé cotton is a lustrous, tightly twisted thread, perfect for creating textured effects. The thread cannot be divided but is available in four different thicknesses, nos. 3, 5, 8 and 12 – the larger the number, the finer the thread.

Variegated and overdyed threads are available in stranded cotton, perlé cotton, wool and silk. The gradual change of shade and colour within one skein of thread, makes these threads ideal for achieving subtle colour variations.

You can also create your own 'variegated' thread by blending plain coloured strands.

Silk threads are available in a large range, from flat untwisted silk to stranded thread and heavy buttonhole thread. They are prized for their very high sheen, but it takes practice to achieve a good result when using this thread type.

If your project will need regular laundering, silk may not be the best choice as some are not colourfast and will easily fade.

Wool yarns are available in a wide variety of thicknesses and a wonderful array of colours. Fine crewel wool is easy to work with and tapestry wool is perfect for heavier stitching. To prevent wearing as you stitch, use short lengths.

Rayon and metallic threads have a spectacular sheen, loved by many embroiderers. However, they have a mind of their own and can be difficult to use. Stitching with short lengths of thread will minimise twisting and tangling.

Metallic threads can be tricky to work with and often wear easily. Make sure you use a needle with a large enough eye to accommodate the thread and use short lengths to make it more manageable.

HINT Choosing colours
Study your surroundings as nature provides many examples of wonderful colour schemes. When you buy threads, ribbons and beads, place your selection on a piece of the fabric you intend to use. Different coloured backgrounds can alter the appearance of the thread colours.

embellishments

Beads and buttons

Beads and buttons are fabulous for adding interest and sparkle to your stitching project.

Beads have been valued and admired throughout history and are an important commodity in many parts of the world. They can be made from many different materials, from shells, wood and seeds to glass, precious metals and stones. Over the last decade bead crafts have become even more popular, which has resulted in a fantastic selection of new and exciting beads being available. They can be threaded onto wire or thread for jewellery or stitched onto fabric for embellishment.

Though the majority of beads are round they come in many other shapes such as cubes, hearts and pear shaped drops. They are also available in a multitude of sizes and finishes in all the colours of the rainbow. Small glass beads, bugle beads and sequins are those most commonly used for embroidery, but crystals, novelty beads and wooden beads are also used to great effect.

Be aware that not all beads are washable and colourfast so choose carefully and test them before decorating a garment that requires regular laundering.

Sequins are available in two main types; flat and faceted. The faceted sequins are slightly cupped which makes them even more reflective than the flat sequins.

The range of colours available is large and though sequins are most commonly round, they are available in other geometric forms and shapes such as stars and hearts.

They are often used in combination with beads and are stitched in place through a hole in the centre and can be placed singly, in rows, or clustered to cover larger areas.

Buttons are traditionally round discs made from bone, shell, metal or wood and later plastic. They can be divided into two main groups; those with two or four holes, through which they are sewn to the fabric and those that have a shank on the back.

There is an endless selection of buttons available in all shapes, sizes and patterns. They vary from quite plain and simple to extraordinary works of art and are fantastic for decorating fabrics. We mainly think of buttons as fasteners in clothing and bed linen, but the earliest buttons were indeed used just as decoration.

Ribbon and braids

Decorative braids and ribbons are available in an array of widths, colours, patterns and textures. As well as being used for embellishment, they can be used for borders, to neaten raw edges and for tying or lacing. Wide ribbons can be used as a fabric, ideal for bookmarks.

Inexpensive craft and satin ribbons are available from most fabric and craft suppliers. Not all ribbons can be laundered so remember to check the ribbon spool for care instructions before you buy.

Ribbons are narrow woven fabric bands. They come in widths from 2mm ($^1/_{16}$") to 10cm (4") in an extensive range of colours, textures, finishes and patterns.

Ribbon can be divided into three main categories, cut-edge, woven-edge and wire-edge.

*Cut edge ribbon*s are made by cutting fabric into narrow strips. The cut edge of the strips are treated with a stiffening agent, which gives them stability and prevents them from fraying. These ribbons are not suitable for projects that get a lot of wear or require laundering, as the edges will wear quickly.

*Woven-edge ribbon*s are woven in narrow strips, giving them a selvedge on each side that will not fray.

*Wire-edge ribbon*s are woven ribbons that have a fine wire woven into the selvedge along each side. This gives the ribbons great flexibility and they can be manipulated into pleats and loops and will hold their shape. Many of these ribbons cannot be washed, so choose carefully.

Braids and cords are made from several threads that are plaited or intertwined to create decorative patterns. They can be made as flat narrow bands or round rope-like cords.

HINT Using wire edge ribbons for stitching
If you don't need the wire in the ribbon edge for your chosen project, simply pull it out very gently from one end of the ribbon.

equipment

sewing tools

Hand stitching and embroidery requires only a few very basic tools. Each project on the following pages has a check list of what you need but it is a good idea to gather some basic equipment for your sewing box before you start.

Scissors

You will need a pair of small, pointed scissors for cutting your threads and a large pair for cutting fabrics.

The most important thing to remember regarding scissors is not to use your embroidery and fabric scissors for anything else! Paper, card and plastic will quickly blunt the blades and ruin your scissors, so use a separate pair for cutting these.

Needles

Needles come in many types and sizes and it is nice to have a good selection at hand.

The size of a needle is given as a number - the higher the number the finer the needle. Ideally the needle should be of similar thickness to the thread you are using. The needle chart below gives you an indication of the various types of needles and their use.

To get started, we suggest you buy a packet of each of the following needles in assorted sizes.

Chenille needles are perfect when you stitch with thicker threads, such as tapestry wool, perlé threads or silk ribbons. They are thicker and have a larger eye than crewel needles.

Crewel or embroidery needles are excellent for most types of embroidery. They have a sharp point and a long eye, which makes them easy to thread.

Sharp or sewing needles are good for general sewing. They have a small round eye that minimises wear on the thread. A fine sharp needle is also good for attaching small beads.

NEEDLE	SIZE	SUITABLE FOR
Chenille A thick needle with a large eye and a sharp tip. This needle was originally used for tufted chenille yarns.	18-24	Suitable for thick threads such as tapestry wool, crewel wool, six strands of stranded cotton, no. 3 and no. 5 perlé cotton, thick silk and heavy metallic thread. Ideal for ribbon and wool embroidery.
Crewel (Embroidery) A finer needle with a large, long eye. The large eye makes the needle easy to thread.	9-10	Suitable for fine embroidery using one or two strands of stranded cotton, silk or rayon. Excellent general purpose needle.
	3-8	Use with three to six strands of stranded cotton, silk or rayon and fine wool, no. 8 and no. 12 perlé cotton and fine metallic thread.
Sharp (Sewing) A good general purpose needle. The small, round eye provides strength for the needle and prevents wear on the thread.	10-12	Suitable for fine embroidery. Use with one or two strands of stranded cotton, silk or rayon. The no. 12 needle is sometimes known as a hand appliqué needle.
	7-9	Use with two or three strands of stranded cotton, silk or rayon.

Pins

A box of dressmaker's pins or glass-headed pins is invaluable for holding tracings or fabrics in place.

Hoops

Hoops are designed to hold the fabric taut while you stitch and are available in many sizes. A hoop is made of two wooden or plastic rings. The fabric is placed between the rings and the outer ring is then tightened to hold the fabric firmly in place. When you buy your hoop, look for a good quality one with a firm bracket, that won't bend when the screw is tightened.

Needle threader

A needle threader is a small tool with a wire loop designed to make it easier to pass the end of a thread through the eye of a needle (see page 17).

Thimble

Although not crucial, a thimble can be useful if you do a lot of stitching or are sewing on thick, firm fabrics, such as denim or leather.

Place the thimble over your middle finger and use it when pushing the needle through the fabric.

Other handy tools

Tape measure and ruler

You will need a tape measure for measuring fabrics. A ruler is essential for ruling straight lines.

Removable tape, magic tape or quilting tape

These are fantastic to use as a guide when stitching straight lines.

tools for transferring

There are many ways to transfer a design onto fabric. It is good to have a small collection of tools on hand for this purpose.

Pens

Fine permanent pen, black or dark brown, is useful for tracing the design onto paper.

Sharp lead pencil or mechanical pencil, is used for tracing directly onto the fabric. Usually the lines will disappear when laundered, but pencil is best used when the lines will be covered completely by stitching. You can also use a very sharp coloured pencil in a shade close to those of your threads.

Fine water-soluble fabric marker is used for tracing directly onto fabric. The pen is ideal if the stitches will not be covering the design lines completely. The marks disappear when the fabric is sponged or rinsed with cold water. It is important not to press the fabric before rinsing because heat will make the pen permanent.

Paper

Tracing paper is essential for tracing the embroidery design from the pattern. Alternatively you can use baking paper for this purpose.

Dressmaker's carbon paper comes in several colours. It is great for thick and dark coloured fabrics with a smooth surface.

Appliqué paper, also known as fusible web, is a very smooth paper with a film of glue on one side. The glue melts when heat is applied. Store appliqué paper in a sealed plastic container or zip lock bag as the glue can dry out and peel away from the paper.

getting started

before you begin

With embroidery, as with most other things, you will achieve a better result if you take the time to read the instructions before you begin and prepare carefully.

How to prepare your fabric

Laundering

Many fabrics will shrink a little when they are laundered for the first time. Dark or bright colours will often contain a little excess dye, which will come out with the first wash. It is therefore a good idea to launder fabrics before you begin stitching to avoid any unpleasant surprises later. Launder your fabric or garment following the manufacturer's care instructions.

Raw edges

When you handle a cut piece of fabric, the edges will loosen and begin to fray. To prevent this happening, neaten the raw edges with a machine zigzag or overlock stitch, or by hand with an overcast stitch.

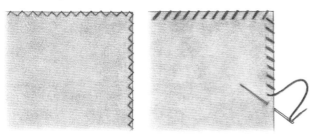

Alternatively fold each side of the fabric twice to enclose the raw edge and tack in place.

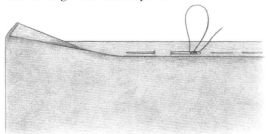

Tacking is a row of temporary stitches used to hold pieces of fabric together or to mark placement guides for positioning your embroidery design. Tacking is best worked using a light coloured machine sewing thread.

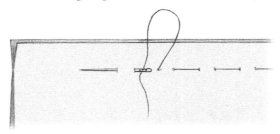

How to prepare your threads

There are a few simple steps to follow when preparing your threads.

Colour fastness

Make sure the threads you are about to use are colourfast. Many threads will have this information on the tag, but it is a good idea to test the thread if you are unsure.

1. Cut off a short length of thread and moisten it.
2. Place the thread on a piece of paper towel or tissue and press between your hands.
3. If the colour bleeds into the paper, the thread is not colourfast.

Using a looped skein

Gently pull out the end of the thread from the centre of the skein.

You can also remove the tags and wind the thread onto a card.

Using a twisted skein

1. Slide the tags off the skein. Untwist and open the skein and cut all the threads at one end.
2. Fold the bundle in half and slide the numbered tag back onto the threads.
3. Divide the threads into three even groups.
4. Plait the threads loosely.
5. Tie the ends with another piece of thread. To remove a strand, simply pull gently from the tag end.

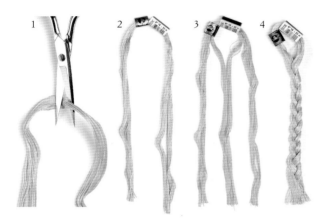

HINT What is a suitable length of thread?
It is best to work with threads no more than 35cm (14"), or the distance from your thumb to your elbow. Longer threads will wear and become tangled easily.

Separating stranded threads

When you need to use more than one strand at a time, it is important to separate the strands and then put them back together. This is known as 'stripping' the thread.

Hold the end of the full six strands between your thumb and index finger.

Ease out a single strand and pull it up and out of the bundle.

The remaining strands will fall back neatly. Repeat for the number of strands needed. Re-group the strands and thread them into the needle.

HINT How to keep the thread untwisted
Threads can often twist as you work. To untwist the threads, let the needle hang freely at regular intervals. The thread will spin back to the correct amount of twist.

Tricks to threading needles

Placing the thread into the eye of a needle need not be a daunting task.

1. Make sure you have cut the end of the thread cleanly. If you have any stray fibres sticking out of the thread tail, they can push the thread away from the needle when you try to thread it.
2. The eye in most needles is elongated; to make the thread fit the eye, flatten the end between your fingers.
3. You can dampen the thread by moistening your fingers and running the end of the thread between them. Trim away the moist piece after threading.

Using a needle threader

1. Bring the wire loop of the needle threader through the eye of the needle.
2. Slip the thread through the wire loop.
3. Pull the threader back out of the eye of the needle, drawing the thread with it.

HINT Needle threading
The eye of a needle has a right and a wrong side. Try turning the needle and thread it from the other side. If you are having real trouble use a larger needle.

Loop method

1. Another method is to fold the thread around the needle.
2. Pinch tightly around the needle and thread and pull the needle up and out.
3. The folded thread will sit between your thumb and index finger.
4. Push the eye end of the needle between your fingers, slipping the eye of the needle onto the the folded thread.

placing & transferring designs

The instructions for each project suggest a method for transferring the design; however you may need to vary the method suggested according to the fabric you have chosen.

Many of the designs have placement guides. When you trace the design remember to include these marks so you can position the design correctly over the fabric.

You will need to photocopy some designs to enlarge them to the correct size. The percentage of enlargement is indicated on each design.

Direct tracing

This method is suitable for light coloured fabrics.

Place a piece of tracing paper over the design and hold it in place with paper clips or removable tape. Use a fine permanent pen to trace the design onto the tracing paper.

Tape the tracing to a window or light box. This step can be omitted for sheer fabrics. Position the fabric over the tracing with the right side facing up. The light shining through will make the design visible through the fabric.

Use a sharp lead pencil or water-soluble fabric marker to trace the design onto the fabric.

To finish

If you have used a water-soluble fabric marker, rinse or sponge the fabric with cold water to remove the marks once the stitching is complete. It is important not to press the fabric before rinsing as the heat will make the pen marks permanent.

Dressmaker's carbon paper

This is a very simple way to transfer designs onto thick and dark fabrics with a smooth surface, such as cotton, silk and linen. Use a paper colour that blends with the colour of your threads as the lines can be permanent.

Place a piece of tracing paper over the design and hold it in place with paper clips or removable tape. Use a fine permanent pen to trace the design onto the tracing paper.

Position the traced design over the fabric and pin in place at the two upper corners. With the coloured side facing the fabric, slide the carbon paper between the fabric and the tracing. Trace over the design lines with a firm, even pressure, using a pencil or ballpoint pen.

Carefully lift one corner of the tracing and carbon paper to make sure all the lines have been transferred before you remove the pins.

Templates

These are a fantastic way to transfer simple shapes that are repeated several times.

1. Draw or trace the shape onto tracing paper with a fine pen. Turn the paper over and retrace the shape with a lead pencil.
2. Place the tracing, with the pen side facing up, over a piece of lightweight card and hold it in place with tape or paper clips.
3. Trace over the shape again, with a firm even pressure, using a pencil or biro. The pencil lines will transfer onto the card.
4. Remove the tracing and cut out the shape from the card, just inside the traced lines.
5. Position the card template onto the fabric and hold it in place while you draw around it with a sharp lead pencil or water-soluble fabric marker.

how to secure your threads

It is important to secure the thread when you start and finish, so that your stitches don't come undone.

When you stitch on articles that require regular laundering, such as clothing, you need to take extra care because laundering can loosen the threads. There are a number of ways to begin and end a thread – the most important thing is to try and avoid unsightly lumps and large knots on the back of your work.

Stitching

This method is quite secure and is suitable for almost any type of embroidery.

1. Begin in an area that will be covered by embroidery and close to the starting point for the stitching. Leave a short tail and take two tiny stitches on the back of the fabric, splitting the first stitch.

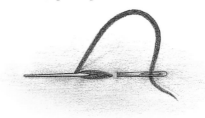

2. Work a few more stitches into the first two to secure the thread firmly. Trim the tail.
3. Finish in a similar way with several small back stitches into the stitches on the wrong side of the fabric, making sure the thread doesn't show on the front.

Weaving

Weaving is suitable only for stitching that will not need laundering as the thread tails can come undone.

1. Leave a 10cm (4") tail of thread hanging on the back of the fabric. After working a small part of the embroidery, re-thread the tail and weave it under the stitches on the back.
2. For added strength, make two or more small stitches into the back of the work. Trim the tail.
3. Finish in the same way.

Knots

Knots

These are easy to use when you have a textured surface, such as thick embroidery, beads and buttons, so the small lump from the knot won't show on the front.

A knot combined with a back stitch is very secure and ideal for embroidered clothing and table linen.

Begin by tying a double knot a short distance from the end of the thread.

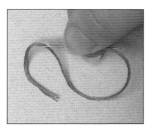

1. Thread the needle. Hold a short tail of thread along the shaft of the needle with the tail towards the eye.

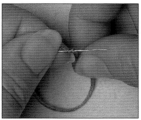

2. Hold the tail and the needle in your left hand. With your right hand, wrap the thread around the point of the needle 2 - 4 times.

3. Holding the wraps between your left thumb and index finger, pull the needle through the wraps. This creates a neat, consistent knot.

4. Finish using one of the methods described previously.

finishing your work

Once the stitching is complete the project will need to be finished. This may involve laundering, or if the fabric or threads are not colourfast or washable, you may need to visit the dry cleaner.

Cleaning

Launder the work by hand in lukewarm water using a mild detergent, or on a gentle machine cycle with the embroidery placed inside a pillowslip. Be careful not to rub the surface of your stitching as that will cause pilling.

Rinse the work thoroughly in clean water. Roll it in a clean towel and press as much excess water out as possible, but do not wring it. Dry the piece flat as quickly as possible, away from direct sunlight.

Pressing

This can make a huge difference to the overall finish of the work. Avoid pressing the right side as this will flatten the threads too much.

Fold a towel into a few thicknesses and place it on your ironing board. Place the work, with the embroidery facing down onto the towel and press the back of the work using a setting appropriate for the fabric. The stitches will sink into the towel and you will be able to press the fabric flat.

need help?

1. *If you prick your finger* and get blood on the fabric, chew a piece of sewing thread or a scrap of fabric and use this to dab off the blood. Your saliva removes your own blood.

2. *If you make a mistake*, don't panic! In most cases, small mistakes are not critical and whether or not to unpick is a personal choice. You can decide to leave the imperfect or incorrect stitching as your artistic rendition. On the other hand, if you know it is going to irritate you every time you look at the piece, take the time to correct it.

   If you decide to unpick, unthread the needle and use the eye-end to pull the stitches out. Don't attempt to stitch back through the fabric.

3. *Don't leave the needle in your work,* as it may rust and leave a mark on the fabric.

4. *If your thread becomes twisted* let the needle hang freely to allow the thread to spin back to the correct amount of twist.

project gallery

Stitches used

Chain stitch, page 74
French knot, page 76
Running stitch, page 77

You will need

Supplies

Turquoise cushion
Turquoise glass beads,
size 6

Stranded cottons

Chocolate brown
Coral
Dark coral
Dark hot pink
Variegated aqua

Equipment

Tracing paper
Dressmaker's carbon
Magic tape
Fine black pen
No. 8 crewel needle

reflection

how to make the cushion

1 **Transferring the design.** Remove the cushion insert from the cover before you begin. See page 85 for the embroidery design.

Trace the design onto tracing paper. Centre the tracing over the cushion front, aligning the base of the stem with the lower edge of the cushion. Pin the tracing in place at the upper corners.

Slide a sheet of dressmaker's carbon under the tracing, making sure the coloured side is facing the fabric. Retrace with a firm pressure to transfer the design onto the fabric.

stitching

2 **Petals.** The petals are worked in chain stitch, using two shades of coral and the dark pink thread. Change between the colours for each petal as indicated on the design, page 85.

Secure the thread and bring it to the front at the base of a petal. Rotate the fabric and work the petal in chain stitch, keeping the stitches short (diag 1).

diag 1

3 **Stem.** Beginning at the base, embroider the stem in chain stitch with three strands of brown thread.

4 **Seeds.** Using three strands of brown thread, stitch a French knot for each seed at the centre of the flower.

5 **Beaded running stitch.** Place a length of magic tape along the upper seam of the cushion cover.

Cut a length of thread 8cm (3 1/4") longer than the width of the cover (diag 2).

diag 2

Secure the thread and bring it to the front at one side, just below the magic tape. Work running stitch along the edge of the tape, threading a bead onto every second stitch (diag 3).

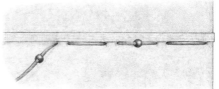

diag 3

Remove the tape. Measure 3cm (1 1/4") from the first row and reposition the tape. Work a second row of beaded running stitch in the same way (diag 4).

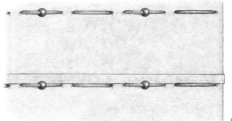

diag 4

Stitch the rest of the full rows in a similar way. Work shorter rows on either side of the flower, finishing each row a short distance from the petals.

HINT Joining a new thread in chain stitch
It can be very frustrating to join a new thread part way through your stitching. With this little hint the join will be seamless.

1. Remove the needle from the old thread, leaving the tail hanging inside the last chain.
2. Secure the new thread on the back and bring it to the front at the same point as the old thread tail.
3. Rethread the old tail into the needle and take it to the back through the same hole in the fabric.

The last chain is now anchored around the new thread.

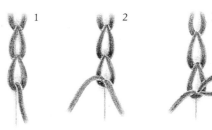

brunch

Techniques used
Attaching buttons, page 80
Fringing, page 80

You will need
Fabrics
Selection of cotton prints
Supplies
White table cloth
Selection of small and medium buttons
Matching machine sewing thread
Equipment
No. 9 sharp needle

how to make the tablecloth

1 Preparing the fabric squares. Cut the fabrics into 3cm (1¼") wide strips. Ease out fabric threads along each long side to make a 3mm (⅛") fringe (diag 1). Repeat for each strip.

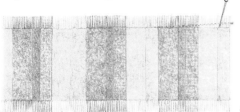

diag 1

Cut the strips into 3cm (1¼") squares. Fringe the remaining two sides of each square in the same way.

The number of fabric squares required will vary according to the size of your tablecloth and how closely you place them.

2 Placing the squares. Lay the tablecloth out flat. Position squares along one side of the tablecloth, spacing them apart and changing the angle of each square. Once you are happy with the arrangement pin the squares in place. Repeat for the remaining sides.

Knot the end of a doubled sewing thread. Bring the thread to the front of a square and remove the pin. Stitch a button in place (diag 2).

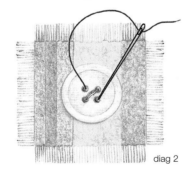

Repeat for the remaining squares around the edge of the tablecloth.

diag 2

HINTS **Fringe and buttons**
You can stitch the squares in place without fringing them first. When the tablecloth is laundered they will begin to fray.

This embellishment makes the table cloth great for outdoor use, because the weight of the buttons will make it hang well.

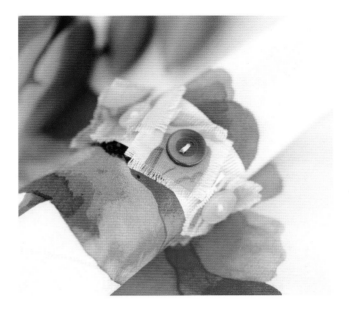

Matching napkin rings. It is very easy to make colourful napkin rings to match your tablecloth.

Cut a 15cm (6") length of 25mm (1") wide firm ribbon such as grosgrain. Place one end of the ribbon over the other to form a circle and stitch in place.

Cover the ribbon circle with fabric squares and buttons in a similar way to the tablecloth, placing them close together.

HINT **How to make a four-cord for attaching buttons**
To speed up the stitching, you can attach the buttons with a four-cord.

1. Fold the sewing thread in half and thread the folded end into the eye of the needle.

2. Double the doubled thread onto itself and tie a knot on the end.

3. Having four threads in the needle means you only have to stitch through the button three times to secure it. Remember to secure the thread on the back.

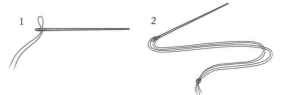

happy feet

Stitches used
Back stitch, page 72
Blanket stitch, page 73
French knot, page 76
Running stitch, page 77
Straight stitch, page 78

Techniques used
Attaching buttons, page 80
Suffolk puff, page 83

You will need
Fabrics
24cm x 30cm wide (9 1/2" x 12") piece of wool felt
for one pair of booties
8cm x 15cm wide (3 1/4" x 6") piece of matching
cotton print for Suffolk puffs
Small piece of wool felt for butterflies, cars
Supplies
60cm (23 5/8") narrow ribbon for the ties
4 x 10mm (3/8") buttons with four holes for wheels
Threads
Stranded cottons to complement the colour
of the felt
Sea green and white for green booties
Cyclamen and orange for red booties
Orange and coral for orange booties
Pistachio green for turquoise booties
Equipment
Tracing paper
Sharp pencil
Water-soluble fabric marker
No. 8 sharp needle
No. 22 chenille needle

how to make the booties

1 **Patterns and templates.** See page 86 for the bootie pattern, embroidery and appliqué templates.

Use the pencil to trace the pattern pieces and placement marks onto tracing paper. Cut out. Use the large needle to pierce holes at the marked positions for the shoelace and at the centre front of the toe piece.

Make a template for your chosen bootie motif in the same way.

2 **Cutting out.** Referring to the cutting layout, trace each bootie piece twice onto the felt and mark the dots through the pierced holes using the fabric marker. Cut out the pieces.

Cutting layout
1. Sole
2. Back
3. Toe

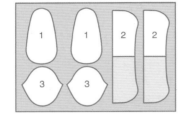

red booties with Suffolk puffs

Trace the circle template twice onto the cotton print and cut out. Prepare two Suffolk puffs following the instructions on page 81.

stitching

Centre a Suffolk puff over a marked dot on a bootie front piece and pin in place. Use the thread tail from the puff to stitch it securely in place (diag 1).

Using two strands of the orange thread, fill the centre of the Suffolk puff with French knots worked close together.

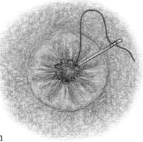

diag 1

green booties with stars

Centre the star template over the marked dot on the bootie front. Trace around the circle with the fabric marker (diag 2). Repeat for the second bootie front piece.

stitching

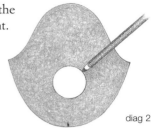

diag 2

Secure two strands of the green thread on the back and bring it to the front on the marked circle. Take the needle to the back at the centre. Work a second straight stitch next to the first, taking the needle to the back through the same hole at the centre (diag 3).

Continue to work straight stitches around the entire circle in this way. Stitch the white highlights, using two strands of thread. Secure the thread and bring it to the front a short distance from the edge of the star. Take the needle to the back halfway along and between two green stitches (diag 4).

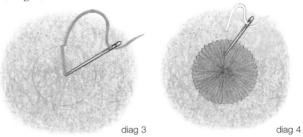

diag 3   diag 4

Continue to work white highlights around the circle in this way, spacing the stitches 3mm ($^1/_8$") apart.

TRY THIS | Make the perfect gift for a special baby
By using the same small designs to decorate hats, singlets or bibs you can easily make a special gift that is sure to be treasured.

orange booties with butterflies

Using the fabric marker, trace the butterfly template twice onto a small piece of felt. Draw a small heart on each wing (diag 5).

diag 5

stitching

Cut out each set of wings after the hearts are embroidered.

Secure two strands of the orange thread and work small back stitches along the drawn lines for the heart on each wing. Cut out.

Work running stitch along the centre of the wings. Pull the thread tightly and secure to gather the wings slightly (diag 6).

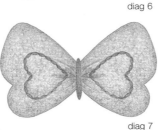

diag 6

Position the wings at the centre of a bootie front and stitch securely in place using the coral thread. Work a long straight stitch along the centre of the wings (diag 7).

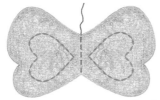

diag 7

Bring the thread to the front to one side of the straight stitch. Work a French knot, taking the needle to the back on the other side of the straight stitch. Work French knots along the length of the straight stitch for the body and work two straight stitches for the antennae (diag 8).

diag 8

turquoise booties with cars

Using the fabric marker, trace the car template twice onto a small piece of felt. Draw a cross on each car to mark the windows and doors (diag 9). Cut out each car.

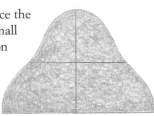

diag 9

stitching

Position a car at the centre front of a bootie piece and pin in place. Using matching thread, stitch the car in place with blanket stitch around the edges. Work back stitch through both layers along the lines for the windows and doors (diag 10).

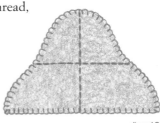

diag 10

For the wheels, position the buttons over the car, aligning the lower pair of holes with the edge of the car. Stitch each button securely in place with a cross stitch (diag 11).

Alternatively, cut four white felt circles, each 1cm (3/8") in diameter for the wheels.

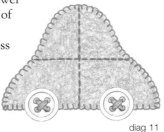

diag 11

HINT Caution when stitching for babies
If you have ever had a baby grab your finger or worse your hair, you will know how hard they can pull. They also love to put things in their mouth so it is very important to stitch things, such as the Suffolk puffs and buttons, very securely in place. To be safe, check the motifs regularly to make sure they are not coming loose.

constructing the booties

Use two strands of thread in a colour to complement the felt to sew the booties together with blanket stitch.

1 **Edging the front and back pieces.** Tie a knot at the end of the thread. Bring it to the front at one side of the upper edge of the bootie front piece. Take the needle to the back through the same hole, leaving a loop. Slide the needle through the loop (diag 1). Pull the thread through, anchoring the loop around the thread.

Take the needle through the felt a short distance from the first stitch. Push it through until the tip appears beyond the felt edge, keeping the thread under the tip of the needle (diag 2).

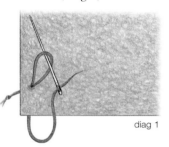
diag 1

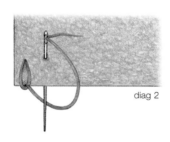
diag 2

Pull the thread through. Work a second blanket stitch around the edge of the felt a short distance from the first (diag 3).

Continue along the edge in this way until reaching the opposite side. After the last stitch, bring the needle to the front through the same hole in the fabric to anchor the last stitch (diag 4). Work a tiny stitch, taking the needle to the back. Secure the thread under the stitches on the back.

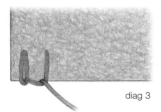
diag 3

diag 4

Work blanket stitch over the upper edge of the remaining front and two back pieces in the same way.

2 **Assembling the booties.** Matching placement marks at the centre front, pin and tack a bootie toe piece to a sole piece (diag 5).

Matching placement marks at the centre back, pin and tack a bootie back to the sole, overlapping the toe piece at the sides (diag 6).

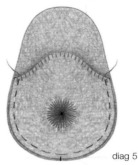

diag 5   diag 6

Secure the thread inside the bootie. Slide the needle between the layers to bring it to the front at the edge (diag 7).

Work blanket stitch in a similar way to the edges of the upper pieces, stitching through all layers around the edge of the bootie to join the upper pieces to the sole (diag 8).

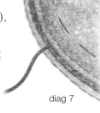
diag 7

Carefully remove the tacking stitches.

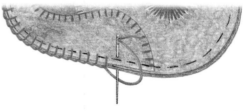
diag 8

3 **Finishing.** Cut the length of ribbon in half. Thread one piece into the large needle. Take the needle to the back at one marked position of the bootie back. Bring the needle to the front at the marked position at the opposite side (diag 9).

Unthread the needle.
Tie the laces in a bow.

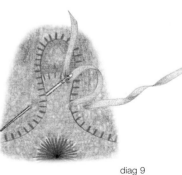
diag 9

day dreams

Stitch used
Attaching sequin with bead

This project requires machine sewing
(Alternatively use a purchased tutu)

You will need

Fabrics

60cm x 240cm wide (23 5/8" x 2yd 22 1/2") white tulle

30cm x 145cm wide (11 3/4" x 1yd 21") white net

Supplies

2m x 35mm wide (2yd 6 3/4" x 1 3/8") dark coral
satin ribbon

Coral machine sewing thread

Gold cup sequins

Coral seed beads

White ballet slippers

Selection of narrow ribbons

Dark coral

Hot pink

Orange

Equipment

No. 9 sharp needle

how to make the tutu

1 **Cutting the tulle.** Cut two circles 9cm (3 1/2") in diameter from one end of the tulle for the bows on the ballet slippers. Straighten the end of the tulle.

constructing the tutu

2 **Gathering.** Using the longest stitch length, stitch along one long edge of the net, 1cm (3/8") from the edge (diag 1).

diag 1

Pulling one thread at one end, gather up the net to measure 68cm (26 3/4"). Even out the gathers (diag 2).

Fold the tulle along the length so it overlaps by 25cm (10"). Pin the fold.

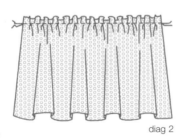

diag 2

Using the longest stitch length, machine stitch 1cm (3/8") from the fold (diag 3).

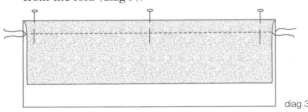

diag 3

Pull one thread and gather the folded edge of the tulle to fit the same size as the net. Even out the gathers. Match the folded edge of the tulle to the gathered edge of the netting and pin in place. Stitch along the previous stitchline (diag 4).

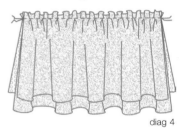

diag 4

3 **Attaching the waist tie.** Fold the wide ribbon in half and mark the fold with a pin. This marks the centre front (diag 5).

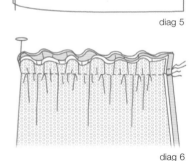

diag 5

Fold the gathered edge of the fabrics in half and mark with a pin (diag 6).

Matching pin marks, pin the ribbon in place along the gathered edge. The edge of the ribbon should be just below the stitch line. Stitch the ribbon in place with a machine zigzag covering the edge of the ribbon (diag 7).

diag 6

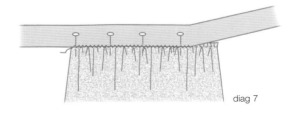

diag 7

Fold the ribbon to the back, over the gathered edge. Pin in place and handstitch to the previous stitchline (diag 8).

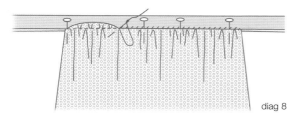

diag 8

4 **Making the bows.** Holding one end of the ribbon, fold a loop over your index finger. Fold a loop over your other index finger (diag 9).

Tie the two loops in a knot, pulling it tight and adjusting the size of the loops to form a bow (diag 10). Trim the tails.

diag 9

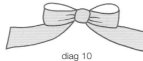

diag 10

5 **Placing and attaching the bows.** Scatter the bows around the edge of the tutu and pin in place through the top layer of the tulle only.

Knot the end of a double sewing thread and bring it to the front through the centre of a bow. Work a stitch through the bow and re-emerge at the centre. Remove the pin (diag 11). Work a second stitch through all layers.

diag 11

Stitch a sequin in place with a seed bead at the centre of the bow (diag 12).

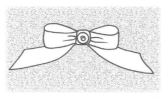

diag 12

From the back, work several stitches into the back of the bow to secure. Repeat for all the remaining bows.

ballet slippers

Remove any bows that may be at the front of the slippers.

Fold each side of a tulle circle to the centre and work a row of gathering across the centre (diag 13).

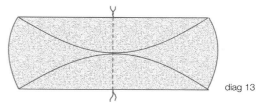

diag 13

Pull up the gathers tightly and take the needle back and forth through the gathers a few times to secure.

Take the needle through the upper edge of a slipper at the centre front (diag 14). Re-emerge through the tulle bow. Take a stitch through the centre of a small bow and stitch in place with a sequin and bead over the tulle bow in the same way as the tutu. Repeat for the remaining slipper.

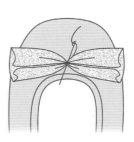

diag 14

TRY THIS Make a matching tiara for your favourite fairy princess by covering a hair band in bows and shimmering crystal beads.

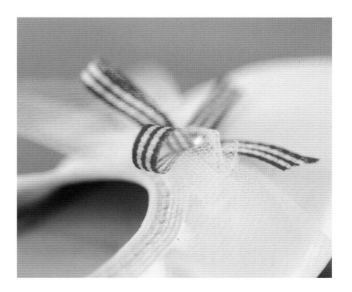

spring

This project requires machine sewing

You will need
Fabric
25cm x 55cm wide (10" x 21⅝") piece of
sea green silk dupion
25cm x 50cm wide (10" x 20") piece of light
pink cotton homespun
Supplies
25cm x 50cm wide (10" x 20") piece of
lightweight fusible wadding eg Pellon
13cm (5") pink plastic handles
Sea green machine sewing thread
80cm (31 ½") light pink ricrac
Pink seed beads
4mm (³⁄₁₆") orange beads
Stranded cottons
Watermelon
Sea green
Variegated no. 8 perlé cotton
Aqua
Equipment
Tracing paper
Dressmaker's carbon
Fine black pen
No. 8 crewel needle
No. 10 crewel needle

The bag measures
19.5cm x 18cm wide (7 ⅝" x 7")
excluding the handles.

how to make the bag

1 Cutting out. Cut the pieces for the bag and handle tabs according to the measurements below. The handle tabs are cut to the correct length after the piece has been folded and pressed.

Silk dupion
Bag, cut one 21cm x 43cm wide (8 1/4" x 17")
Handle tabs, cut one 22cm x 6cm wide (8 5/8" x 2 3/8")

Cotton homespun and wadding
Bag, cut one 21cm x 43cm wide (8 1/4" x 17")

Cutting layout

1. Bag
2. Handle tabs

Silk dupion   Cotton homespun and wadding

2 Preparing the fabric for embroidery. See page 87 for the embroidery design.

Place the wadding with the soft side facing up, over the wrong side of the silk. Fuse in place with a warm dry iron. Leave the fabric on a flat surface to cool. Using a machine zigzag, stitch the layers together along all edges (diag 1).

Trace the design onto tracing paper, marking the centre of each flower with a dot. Position the tracing over the silk, aligning it with the upper edge of the fabric and the placement marks with the straight grain. Pin in place at the upper corners. Slide a piece of dressmaker's carbon under the tracing, with the coloured side facing the fabric (diag 2). Retrace along the design lines to transfer the design.

diag 1

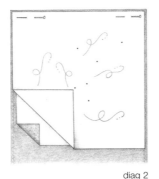

diag 2

stitching

3 Scrolls. Use the perlé thread in the large needle. Begin at the base of a scroll and stitch along the marked line in chain stitch (diag 3).

diag 3   diag 4

Secure the last stitch and work two French knots at the tip of the scroll (diag 4).

Use three strands of the sea green stranded cotton and work back stitch along the centre of the chain stitches following the instructions on page 42. Stitch the other four scrolls in the same way.

4 Blossom. Use a single strand of matching pink thread in the small needle to stitch the ricrac flowers, following the step-by-step instructions. Using two strands of melon thread, bring it to the front at the centre of a flower. Take the needle to the back through the edge of the ricrac to work a straight stitch between two petals (diag 5).

diag 5

Bring the thread to the front just outside the edge of the ricrac. Thread on a seed bead. Take the needle to the back through the edge of the ricrac, sharing the same hole as the straight stitch (diag 6). Repeat between each petal.

diag 6

Stitch a large orange bead at the centre of the flower (diag 7).

diag 7

Back stitch over chain stitch

1. Bring the thread to the front inside the first chain. Take the needle to the back at the end of the row.

2. Bring the thread to the front inside the second chain. Take the needle to the back inside the first chain, sharing the hole of the first back stitch.

3. Continue to work a back stitch into every chain in this way.

TRY THIS Decorate the bag with gathered ribbon flowers similar to those on the canister on page 54.

constructing the bag

All seam allowances are 1.5cm (⅝") unless otherwise specified. The shaded areas on the following diagrams indicate the right side of the fabric.

Bag

1. Fold the embroidered piece in half across the width, with right sides together and matching raw edges. Pin and stitch the side seams (diag 1).

diag 1

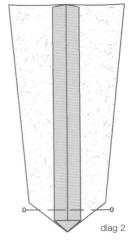

diag 2

2. Finger press the side seams open. Mark the fold with a pin at each side. Open one corner and fold the side seam aligning it with the pin (diag 2).

3. Measure 2cm (¾") from the tip of the corner. Pin and stitch across the corner (diag 3). Repeat for the remaining corner.

4. Push the corner point towards the base of the bag and handstitch the tip to the wadding to hold it in place (diag 4). Turn the bag to the right side.

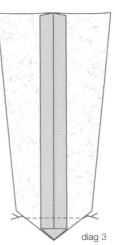

diag 3

diag 4

Handle tabs

5. Fold the piece in half along the length and press (diag 5). Unfold.

diag 5

6. Fold one long side, aligning the raw edge with the foldline. Press the fold (diag 6). Repeat for the opposite side.

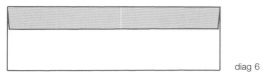

diag 6

7. Refold the piece along the length, enclosing the raw edges and press (diag 7).

diag 7

8. Cut four 5.5cm (2 1/4") pieces from the folded strip for the handle tabs.

Attaching the handle

9. Measure 2.5cm (1") from each side seam and mark with pins (diag 8). Match the pin marks on the opposite side of the bag.

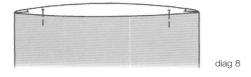

diag 8

10. Matching the raw edges, place a handle tab over the bag, aligning the outer edge with a pin. Pin and stitch in place (diag 9). Repeat for the remaining three handle tabs.

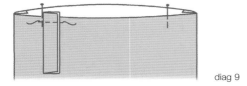

diag 9

11. Place a handle over the bag and loop the handle tabs through the handle. Matching raw edges pin and stitch the other end of each handle tab in place (diag 10). Repeat for the other side of the bag.

12. Fold the upper edge of the bag to the inside and press the fold. Topstitch 3mm (1/4") from the folded edge around the upper edge (diag 11).

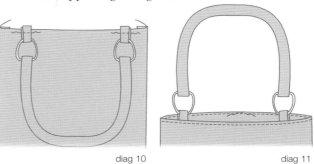

diag 10   diag 11

Making the lining

13. Make the lining in the same way as the bag. Fold and press the seam allowance around the upper edge of the lining to the wrong side.

Finishing

14. With wrong sides together and matching side seams, place the lining inside the bag. Pin in place.

15. Handstitch the lining in place around the upper edge, sliding the needle between the layers (diag 12).

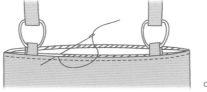

diag 12

impressions

braids and
beads

embroidery

braids and beads

Technique used
Attaching beads, page 72

You will need
Supplies
White shirt
2m (2yd 6 ¾") red
Russian braid
Small coral glass beads
Orange/pink seed beads
Red machine sewing thread
Equipment
Tracing paper
Fine black pen
Sharp pencil
No. 9 sharp needle
No. 10 crewel needle

embroidery

Stitches used
Detached chain, page 75
French knot, page 76
Running stitch, page 77

You will need
Supplies
White shirt
No. 8 variegated perlé
cottons
Dark coral
Pale apricot
Equipment
Tape measure
Sharp pencil
No. 8 crewel needle

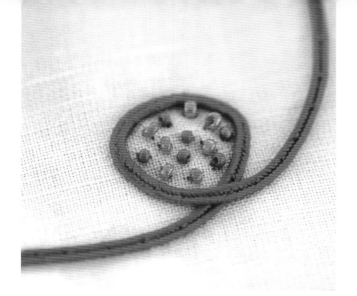

how to embellish with braids and beads

1 **Transferring the design.** See page 88 for the embroidery design.

Using the pen, trace the design onto the tracing paper. Position the tracing over a window or light box and tape in place. Place the left hand side of the shirt front over the tracing and tape in place. Use the sharp pencil to retrace the design onto the shirt.

2 **Preparing the braid.** The braid is stitched in place using doubled matching sewing thread in the larger needle.

Knot the end of the thread. Slide the needle inside the braid, emerging a short distance from the end (diag 1).

diag 1

Pull the knot inside the braid with a short tug.

Wrap the thread several times around the braid. Take the needle through the wrapping twice to secure (diag 2).

Trim the braid close to the wrapping.

diag 2

stitching

3 **Attaching the braid.** Place the shirt front flat on a table while you stitch. Position the wrapped end of the braid at the point marked with a star on the pattern and secure with two small stitches worked over the end and into the wrapping (diag 3).

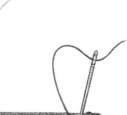

diag 3

Place the braid along the marked line and bring the thread to the front through the centre of the braid. Take a small back stitch along the centre (diag 4).

Keeping the shirt as flat as possible, continue to stitch the braid in place with small back stitches along the centre, shaping it as you stitch. Overlap the braid where necessary to follow the flow of the design (diag 5).

diag 4

4 **Beading.** The beads are stitched in place one at a time, using doubled thread in the small needle. Mix the two types of beads and stitch them in place randomly.

Fill five circles closely with beads, changing the direction of the beads as you stitch them in place one at a time (diag 6).

Stitch the beads in place further apart in the remaining four loops.

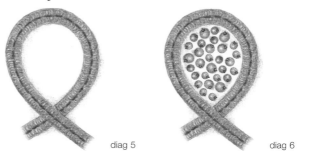

diag 5   diag 6

| TRY THIS | Imagine how fantastic a similar scroll design would look stitched onto a cushion or throw. |

how to embellish with embroidery

1 **Preparing the shirt.** Fold the collar in half and mark the centre back with a pin (diag 1).

Using the pencil, mark a small dot at the edge of the collar at the centre back and at 5cm (2") intervals towards the front on each side. Remove the pin.

diag 1

stitching

2 **Buttonhole decoration.**
Secure the dark coloured thread and bring it to the front just above a buttonhole. Work a long detached chain (diag 2).
Stitch another six detached chains around one side of the buttonhole, finishing at the opposite end (diag 3).

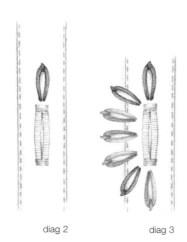

diag 2   diag 3

Stitch around the remaining buttonholes in the same way, alternating between the colours.

Using a contrasting colour to the detached chains, secure the thread behind the corresponding button and work three stitches through the holes in the button (diag 4).

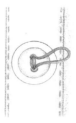

diag 4

3 **Collar.** When you work the stitching on the collar, slide the needle between the layers of fabric to keep the underside of the collar looking neat.

Using light apricot, work a detached chain along each side of the collar tip (diag 5). Stitch a third detached chain half way between the first two.

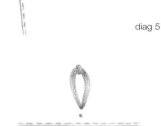

diag 5

Stitch three detached chains around each of the marked positions. Work the centre stitch in each group first at a right angle to the edge of the collar (diag 6).

diag 6

Using dark coral, begin at one collar tip and work a French knot.
Sliding the needle between the layers of fabric, work running stitch, 6mm (1/4") from the edge of the collar to the next group of detached chains (diag 7).
Stitch a French knot at the marked position. Continue around the edge of the collar in this way.

diag 7

twilight

Stitch used
French knot, page 76

You will need
Supplies
Ivory shawl
5.5m x 7mm wide (6yd x $5/16$")
of grey variegated silk ribbon
Ivory stranded cotton
Equipment
Fine water-soluble fabric marker
Dressmaker's pins
No. 9 crewel needle

How to embellish the shawl

1 **Preparing the shawl.** Place one end of the shawl flat on the table. Using the water-soluble fabric marker, draw a trailing line across the end of the shawl (diag 1). Repeat at the opposite end of the shawl.

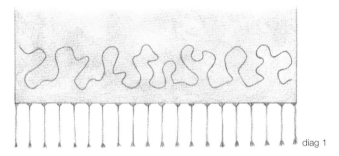

diag 1

2 **Placing the ribbon.** Cut the length of ribbon in half. Fold one end of one length to the back. Place the folded end on the marked line at one side of the shawl and pin in place (diag 2).

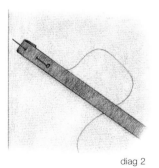

diag 2

diag 3

Continue to pin the ribbon in place along the marked line, folding it back on itself to turn the curves (diag 3). As you near the opposite side, trim the ribbon, allowing 1cm (³⁄₈") to be folded under.

stitching

3 **French knots.** Secure two strands of thread and take it to the front at one side of the shawl, through the folded end of the ribbon. Work a French knot through all layers (diag 4).

diag 4

Bring the thread to the front in the centre of the ribbon a short distance from the first knot (diag 5). Stitch a second knot, taking care not to pull the thread tight across the back.

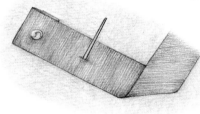

diag 5

Continue to stitch French knots along the centre of the ribbon at regular intervals. Take care not to pull the thread taut between the knots and remove the pins as you stitch.

diag 6

Adjust the spacing of the knots as you work, to make sure a knot is placed at the centre of the turns in the ribbon (diag 6).

Work the last knot through the folded end of the ribbon at the opposite side.

| TRY THIS | For a truly sparkling evening shawl, stitch the ribbon in place with contrasting seed beads or replace the ribbon with a row of overlapping |

sequins following the step-by-step instructions on page 77.

first prize

Stitch used
French knot, page 76

Techniques used
Attaching buttons, page 80
Gathered ribbon flower, page 81

You will need
Supplies
Girl's cardigan
One piece each of red and white wool felt
75cm x 15mm wide (30" x 5/8") red ribbon
with white spots
45cm x 15mmm wide (18" x 5/8") white ribbon
with black dots
1m x 6mm wide (1yd 3 3/8" x 1/4") black and
white check ribbon
Nine 12mm (1/2") pearl buttons
Threads
Red stranded cotton
Matching machine sewing thread
Equipment
Tissue paper
Tracing paper
Fine black pen
Fine water-soluble fabric marker
No. 5 crewel needle
No. 8 sharp needle

how to embellish the cardigan

1 **Preparing the felt pieces.** See page 89 for the embroidery design and felt template.

Trace the felt template onto the tracing paper and cut out. Using the fabric marker, trace the template four times onto the red felt and five times onto the white. Cut out the flowers.

2 **Preparing the ribbon flowers.** Cut the red and the white spotted ribbon into 15cm (6") lengths. Make a gathered flower from each piece.

3 **Transferring the design.** Using the pen, trace the embroidery design and placement marks for the sleeve onto the tissue paper. Centre the tracing over the left hand sleeve, aligning the placement marks with the centre of the sleeve and pin in place (diag 1).

Using a contrasting sewing thread, tack along the design line. Mark the position for each flower with a cross stitch. Lightly moisten the tissue paper with a damp sponge. Wait a few moments before carefully tearing the paper away, leaving the tacking in the fabric (diag 2).

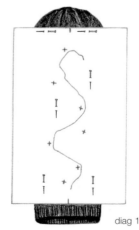 

diag 1   diag 2

HINT You can prepare and arrange the flowers on the sleeve before stitching the ribbon in place.

stitching

4 Check ribbon scroll.
Fold one end of the ribbon to the back and pin the folded end in place at the end of the tacked line. Twist the ribbon twice and pin in place along the line (diag 3).

diag 3

Continue to twist the ribbon in the same direction and pin in place along the marked line, placing a pin after each full twist. When reaching the opposite end, trim the ribbon and fold the end under.

Using six strands of the red stranded cotton in the large needle, secure the thread and bring it to the front through the folded end of the ribbon.

Work a French knot. Emerge at the position of the next pin, between the twists in the ribbon. Remove the pin and work a French knot to secure the ribbon, taking care not the pull the thread tight between the stitches (diag 4).

diag 4

Continue to work a French knot between each ribbon twist, removing the pins as you work. Take care not to tighten the thread between stitches. Finish with a French knot through the folded end of the ribbon.

5 Ribbon flowers.
Position a gathered red ribbon flower over a white felt flower and stitch in place around the gathered edge (diag 5). Unthread the needle, leaving the thread tail on the back. Repeat for the remaining four flowers. Stitch the white ribbon flowers to the red felt flowers in the same way.

diag 5

Using the thread tails, stitch seven of the flowers securely in place on the sleeve, by working several stitches through the centre (diag 6).

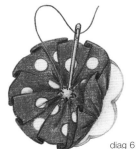

diag 6

Stitch the remaining two flowers in place on the right hand front of the cardigan.

Using two strands of red thread, stitch a button in place at the centre of each flower.

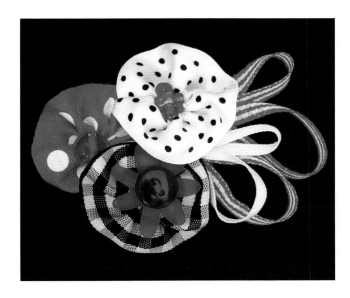

Ribbon flower brooch

1. Cut a circle of felt 3cm (1 1/4") in diameter.

2. Make three gathered ribbon flowers and stitch in place on the felt circle. Stitch a button or beads at the centre of each ribbon flower.

3. Loop short lengths of narrow ribbon and stitch in place in and around the gathered flowers.

4. Stitch a brooch pin securely in place on the back of the felt.

poppy

Techniques used
Fringing, page 80
Gathered flower, page 81
Ricrac flower, page 82

You will need

Fabrics

15cm x 30cm wide (6" x 12") piece of natural coloured linen

Supplies

35cm x 15mm wide (13 3/4" x 5/8") red and cream wire edge ribbon

70cm x 6mm wide (27 1/2" x 1/4") red and white check ribbon

30cm x 6mm wide (11 3/4" x 1/4") red and white ribbon

24cm x 15mm wide (9 1/2" x 5/8") red ricrac

3 small black beads

3 black sequins

Three 12mm (1/2") black buttons

Black stranded cotton

Small can

Equipment

Tracing paper

Sharp pencil

Craft glue

Red machine sewing thread

how to cover the canister

How to work out the size for your cover.

To determine the size of the fabric you need to cover your can you need to do the following.

Measure the hight of the can and add 1cm (³/₈") for the fringe (A). Measure the circumference of your can using a tape measure. Add 3cm (1¹/₄") for the overlap and fringe (B).

1 Cutting out. Cutting along the grain, cut out your fabric measuring A x B wide (diag 1).

Ease out threads along one long and one short side to create a 1cm (³/₈") fringe.

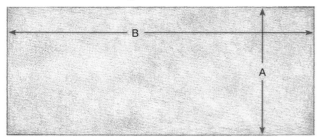

diag 1

2 Transferring the design. See page 84 for the stitching design. Using the pencil, trace the outlines and mark the placement for the flowers onto the tracing paper. Cut out the tracing along the marked lines.

Aligning the edges, position the tracing over the fabric. Pin in place. Using the pencil, pierce holes at the marked positions for the flowers and mark onto the fabric with a dot. Remove the tracing (diag 2).

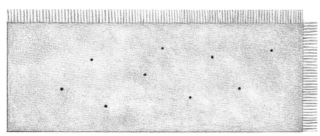

diag 2

HINT	If your can is a lot larger than the one shown, you may wish to make more flowers or place them further apart.

stitching

3 Gathered flowers. Cut the widest ribbon into three even lengths. Gently remove the wire from one edge (see hint). Gather each length into a flower.

Using doubled red sewing thread, stitch the centre of each flower in place at the marked positions. Bring the needle to the front in the centre of a flower and thread a sequin onto the needle. Centering the sequin, work a stitch over one side and emerge at the opposite side (diag 3).

diag 3

diag 4

Take the needle to the back through the hole and emerge outside the sequin, halfway between the previous stitches (diag 4). Work a stitch into the centre. Place a fourth stitch at the remaining quarter mark.

4 Looped ribbon flowers. Cut the red and white check ribbon into 23cm (9") lengths. Secure the thread and bring it to the front at one of the marked positions. Stitch one end of one ribbon securely in place. With the thread on the back, fold the ribbon into a small loop. Bring the thread to the front at the centre, through the ribbon. Take the needle back through the ribbon to secure the loop (diag 5).

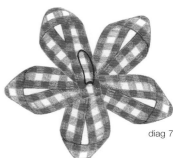

diag 5

Fold the ribbon back on itself in the direction for the next loop. Bring the needle to the front at the centre through the folded ribbon. Make a second ribbon loop, the same size as the first and secure in the same way as before (diag 6). Continue to fold and secure ribbon loops to form five or six petals (diag 7). Trim the ribbon.

Attach a black button in the centre of the ribbon loops for the flower centre.

diag 6   diag 7

5 Ricrac flowers. Cut the ricrac into three even lengths. Secure the thread and bring it to the front at one of the marked positions. Stitch the ricrac in place to form the petals.

Using two strands of black thread, work a straight stitch between each petal. Stitch a black bead in place at the centre.

6 Covering the canister. Apply a small amount of glue around the upper and lower edge of the can and in a line down one side. Leave for a few moments to allow the glue to become sticky (diag 8).

Place the unfringed end of the fabric over the line of glue and, ensuring the fabric is straight along the upper and lower edges, roll it tightly around the canister (diag 9).

diag 8

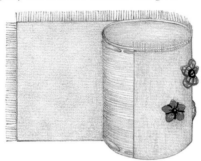

diag 9

Apply a small amount of glue along the back of the overlapping end, just back from the fringed edge (diag 10). Leave the glue to become sticky to prevent it from seeping through before smoothing the fabric down. Apply a small amount of glue around the lower edge of the covered canister and glue the narrow ribbon in place around the base.

diag 10

HINT Using wire edge ribbon
Many beautiful ribbons are wire edged. To use these for gathered ribbon flowers you first need to remove the wire.

Cut the ribbon to the required length and ease the cut end of the ribbon back from the wire.

Hold the tip of the wire firmly and gently ease it out of the ribbon edge.

garnish

You will need
Supplies
Black apron
Black oven mit
No. 8 varigated perlé cotton
Coral red
Equipment
Tracing paper
White dressmaker's carbon
Fine pen
No. 8 crewel needle

how to embellish the apron and oven mitt

1 Transferring the designs. See page 90 for the embroidery design.

Enlarge the design for the apron and trace onto tracing paper. Centre the tracing at a slight angle over the apron, centering the word 'chef'. Pin the tracing in place at two corners. Slide a piece of dressmaker's carbon under the tracing with the coloured side facing the fabric. Use a sharp pencil and retrace the design with an even pressure to transfer the design.

Using a chalk pencil draw a trailing line from each end of the word on the apron.

Trace and transfer the design in the size given onto the oven mitt in a similar way.

2 Stitching. Secure the thread on the back of the apron at one end of the marked line.

Work stem stitch along the line, keeping the stitches an even length. Shorten the stitches slightly when stitching around tight curves to achieve a smooth line.

To begin a new length of thread, choose a section of the thread that is close to the colour of the last stitch (diag 1).

diag 1

When you reach the pocket, keep one hand inside the pocket and continue to stitch through the pocket only (diag 2).

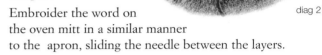

diag 2

Embroider the word on the oven mitt in a similar manner to the apron, sliding the needle between the layers.

HINT **Joining a new thread in stem stitch**
You can achieve an invisible join in your stem stitch by following these easy steps.

1. Leaving the last stitch very loose, take the thread to the front of your work a short distance away from the area being stitched Unthread the needle leaving the thread tail hanging.

1.

2. Secure the new thread on the back and bring it to the front, half way along the last stitch.

2.

3. Gently pull the old thread tail, pulling the last stitch taut. Turn the work over, pull the old thread to the back and secure.

4. Continue working the row of stem stitch with the new thread.

spots

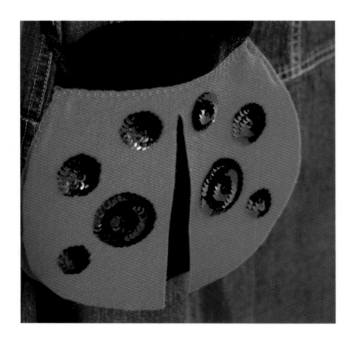

Stitches used
Blanket stitch, page 73
Row of sequins, page 77

Technique used
Plaiting, page 81

You will need
Two pieces each of red and black felt
24cm x 30cm wide (9 1/2" x 12")
6mm (1/4") black cup sequins
Black seed beads
Black machine sewing thread
3m (3yd 10") of thin black cord
Red no. 8 perlé thread
Equipment
Tracing paper
Sharp pencil
Fine water-soluble fabric marker
Craft glue
No. 8 crewel needle
No. 10 crewel needle

how to make the bag

1 **Cutting out.** See pages 92 and 93 for the bag pattern. Trace the pattern pieces and spots onto tracing paper.

Cut holes for the spots on the wing piece before cutting out the paper pattern piece.

Position the wing piece over the red felt and pin in place. Using the fabric marker, trace the spots and cutting lines. Repeat for a second wing piece (diag 1).

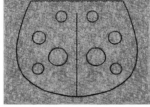

diag 1

Cut out the wing pieces along the marked cutting lines after stitching the spots.

Position the bag piece over the black felt and pin in place. Cut out along the edge of the pattern. Repeat for a second piece.

stitching

2 **Medium spots.** Secure a doubled black thread and bring it to the front on the marked line for one spot. Place a black sequin on the line and stitch in place with a back stitch (diag 2).

Continue to stitch overlapping sequins in place around the circle. When you near the starting point, bring the thread to the front at the edge of the first sequin and stitch the second-to-last sequin in place with a back stitch as before (diag 3).

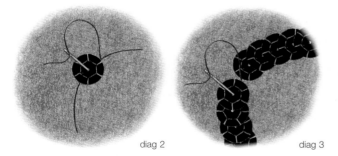

diag 2   diag 3

Bring the thread to the front under the first sequin. Work a back stitch into the last sequin and slide it into place under the first (diag 4).

diag 4

Bring the needle to the front 3mm ($^1/8$") inside the first circle of sequins (diag 5). Stitch the second circle in place in the same way as the first.

To finish, bring the thread to the front at the centre. Thread on a sequin followed by a seed bead. Take the needle over the seed bead and back through the sequin to secure (diag 6).

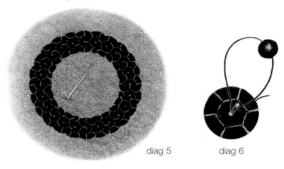

diag 5   diag 6

3 **Large spot.** Fill the circle for the large spot in a similar way, working three concentric circles of overlapping sequins and finishing with a single sequin in the centre.

4 **Small spot.** Stitch the outer circle of overlapping sequins in the same way as the other circles. Bring the thread to the front inside the first circle, 3mm ($^1/8$") from the sequins. Fill the centre of the circle with six overlapping sequins stitched in place in a small circle.

constructing the bag

5 **Attaching the wing piece to the bag.** Position a wing piece over a bag piece, curving it slightly as indicated on the pattern and pin in place along the upper edge. Rotate the bag so the top is facing you.

Using the red perlé thread and the larger needle, bring the thread to the front through the black felt at the left hand edge of the wing piece (diag 7).

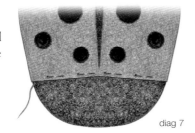

diag 7

Work a 6mm (1/4") straight stitch at a right angle to the edge, through all layers. Re-emerge through the same hole at the edge of the wing piece (diag 8).

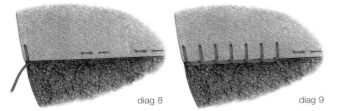

diag 8   diag 9

Work 6mm (1/4") long and wide blanket stitches over the upper edge of the wing piece, removing the pins as you stitch (diag 9).

Repeat for the second wing and bag piece.

6 **Making the bag.** Place the front and back bag pieces with wrong sides together and matching edges. Pin in place around the edge, keeping the wings out of the way. Starting just below the upper edge of the wings, machine stitch around the edge of the bag, 6mm (1/4") from the edge (diag 10).

diag 10

Reposition the wing pieces and pin in place along the side seams.

Using the red thread, blanket stitch through all layers from the upper edge of the wing piece 4cm (1 1/2") along each side seam (diag 11).

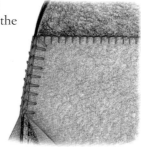

diag 11

7 **Making the plaited strap.** Cut the black cord into three equal lengths. Tie the lengths of cord together and secure or get someone to hold it for you while you plait. Plait the three cords and tie a knot at the opposite end to secure.

Thread black doubled machine sewing thread into the small needle and knot the end. Take the needle through the end of the plait (diag 12).

diag 12   diag 13

Tug the thread to pull the knot into the plait. Wrap the thread tightly and closely around the plait for 1cm (3/8"). Take the needle through the wrapping several times to secure (diag 13). Cut the thread.

Trim the knotted end of the plait a short distance from the wrapping. Repeat at the opposite end of the strap. Apply a small amount of glue to the cut ends of the strap and leave to dry.

8 **Attaching the strap.** Using doubled machine sewing thread, stitch one end of the strap securely in place inside the bag along the side seam (diag 14). Repeat for the opposite end, making sure the strap is not twisted.

diag 14

| HINT | You can also make the spots on the wings from circles of black felt and stitch them in place with blanket stitch around the edge. |

snug as a bug

Stitches uses

Blanket stitch, page 73
Chain stitch, page 74
Running stitch, page 77

Technique used

Appliqué, page 79

You will need

Cream satin bound cot blanket

Fabrics

Three pieces of red wool felt
One piece of black wool felt
Three pieces of brown wool felt
30cm x 80cm wide (12" x 31 1/2") piece of white tulle

Supplies

2m x 20mm wide (2yd 6 3/4" x 3/4") yellow satin ribbon
25cm x 90cm wide (10" x 35 1/2") piece of appliqué paper
White machine sewing thread

No. 8 perlé cottons

Black
Dark brown
Pale gold
Red
Yellow

Equipment

Craft glue
Fabric sealer eg Fray-stop
Sharp pencil
Fine water-soluble fabric marker
Tracing paper
No. 8 crewel needle
No. 8 sharp needle

how to decorate the blanket

1 **Preparing the appliqué pieces.** See page 91 for the appliqué templates.

Trace the template for the ladybird's spots twelve times onto appliqué paper. Trace the remaining templates three times each onto separate pieces of appliqué paper.

2 **Cutting out.** Fuse the pieces of appliqué paper to the appropriate felt pieces. Cut out along the marked cutting lines and remove the backing paper.

Using a 24cm (9 1/2") diameter plate as a template, trace three circles onto the tulle and cut out for the wings.

HINT Using appliqué paper to transfer the templates onto the felt is easier than trying to trace the template pieces. It also stabilises the felt a little so it doesn't stretch or distort when you stitch it in place.

---

stitching

The spots and stripes are stitched onto the red and brown felt pieces before they are stitched onto the blanket.

3 **Ladybird spots.** Position four spots with the glue side facing down, onto the right side of each red felt piece and fuse in place. Using the black thread, work blanket stitch around the edge of each spot. Complete each circle of stitches following step 5 for blanket stitch pinwheel to achieve a neat finish.

4 **Bee stripes.** Cut the yellow ribbon into 16cm (6 1/4") lengths. Apply four lines of glue, evenly spaced across the right side of each brown felt piece (diag 1).

Position a length of ribbon over each line of glue for the stripes (diag 2).

diag 1

diag 2

Trim the ends of each ribbon along the edge of the felt and apply a small amount of fabric sealer to each end. Leave to dry.

Using the yellow thread, work a row of running stitch along each side of each ribbon. Bring the brown thread to the front at the end of the stitching. Slide the eye-end of the needle under the first yellow stitch (diag 3).

diag 3

Pull the thread through. Slide the needle under the second stitch in the same direction (diag 4).

diag 4

Continue to wrap the brown thread into the yellow stitches to the end of the row (diag 5). Repeat for all the ribbon stripes.

diag 5

5 **Stitching the bees and ladybirds onto the blanket.** Pin the wings and heads for the ladybirds together before you place them onto the blanket.

Using the diagram as a guide, arrange the bees and ladybirds on the blanket and pin each piece in place (diag 6). Do not fuse.

diag 6

Ladybirds. Remove the wing piece from each ladybird and set aside. Using matching thread, stitch the heads in place with blanket stitch worked over the upper curved edge (diag 7).

diag 7

Reposition the wing pieces and pin in place. Using the red thread, stitch the wings in place with blanket stitch around the edges.

Using the fabric marker, rule a line along the centre of each wing piece and draw the antennae onto the blanketing (diag 8).

Using the black thread, stitch along each line in chain stitch.

Bees. Using the brown thread, stitch each bee in place with blanket stitch.

diag 8

Draw the antennae in the same way as the ladybird and stitch in chain stitch using brown thread.

Fold a tulle circle in half. Using the sewing thread, work gathering stitches across the centre (diag 9). Pull the thread to gather the tulle tightly.

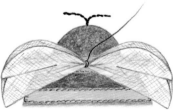

diag 9

Position the wings just below the bee's head, with the folded edge towards the tail. Pin and stitch in place (diag 10). Repeat for the remaining wings.

Using pale gold thread, work a trail behind each bee in long running stitches.

diag 10

HINT **Wool or acrylic felt**
It is better to use wool felt than acrylic craft felt for stitching projects. Wool felt can be ironed, but acrylic felt will melt very easily under the iron. If you are unable to purchase wool felt, do not use appliqué paper for your projects.

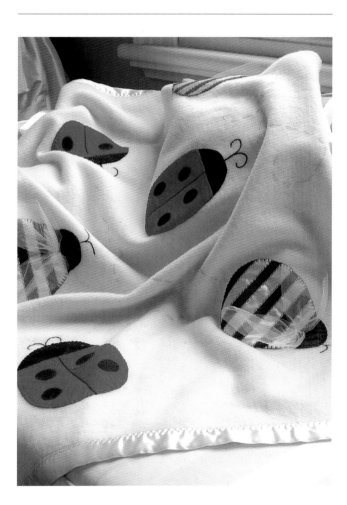

Stitches used

Cross stitch, page 74
Feather stitch, page 75
French knot, page 76
Herringbone stitch, page 76
Running stitch, page 77

This project requires
machine sewing

You will need

Fabrics
Two pieces of brown felt
Supplies
1m x 15mm wide
(1yd 3 3/8" x 5/8") yellow
ribbon for the tie
Black satin ribbon with
cream edge
Brown satin ribbon
Green satin ribbon
Red satin ribbon
Yellow ribbon
No. 8 perlé cottons
Black
Red
Equipment
Craft glue
Fabric sealer eg Fray-stop
Pencil
Ruler
No. 8 crewel needle

journey

how to make the notebook cover

1 How to determine the size for your book cover.
Measure the book from the centre of the spine to the front edge (diag 1).

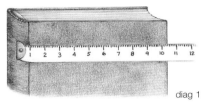

diag 1

Add 10cm (4") to this measurement for the flap to go around the front edge of the book and the seam allowance along the spine. This measurement is the width of each felt piece (A).

Measure the length of the book and add 1.5cm (⁵/₈") for the seam allowance at the upper and lower edges. This measurement is the depth of each felt piece (B). Cut out your felt pieces measuring B x A wide (diag 2).

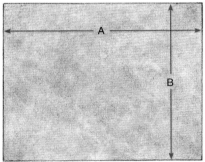

diag 2

2 Preparing the front piece. Set the wide yellow satin ribbon aside for the tie. Cut the remaining ribbons into lengths matching the width of the felt piece (diag 3).

diag 3

Apply a small amount of fabric sealer to each end of the short ribbon pieces and leave to dry. Place the long yellow ribbon temporarily across the centre of the felt. Arrange the short ribbons on each side of the yellow ribbon (diag 4). Remove the long yellow ribbon and set aside.

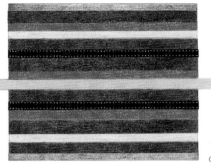

diag 4

Lift a short piece of ribbon and apply a line of glue onto the felt (diag 5). Reposition the ribbon, but do not press down as the glue might seep through. Repeat for the remaining short pieces and leave to dry.

diag 5

stitching

3 Embroidering over the ribbons. Work the stitching using three strands of thread. Change the thread colour and type of stitch you use on each ribbon.

Running stitch can be worked just in from the edge along each side of the wider ribbons or along the centre of a narrow ribbon.

French knots. Place the ruler along the centre of the ribbon and use a sharp pencil to mark a small dot at regular intervals. Stitch a French knot at each marked position (diag 6).

diag 6

Cross stitch. Mark the ribbon with dots along the centre in the same way as the French knots. Work each cross stitch so it is centred over the dot.

Herringbone stitch is worked across the full width of the ribbon, taking the needle through the layers just in from the ribbon edges (diag 7).

diag 7

Feather stitch is worked across the full width of the ribbon in a similar way to the herringbone stitch.

| TRY THIS | For a more feminine book cover, use lace, ribbons and pretty braids in pastel colours. |

constructing the book cover

4 Making the cover. With right sides together and matching edges, place the second felt piece over the front piece. Pin and stitch along the left hand side, leaving a 1.5cm (⁵⁄₈") seam allowance (diag 8).

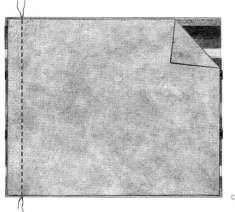

diag 8

Unfold and finger press the seam open.

With the wrong side of the cover facing up, fold 8.5cm (3 ³⁄₈") to the back at each side for the flaps and pin in place. Work a row of small running stitches along the upper and lower edge to secure the flaps (diag 9).

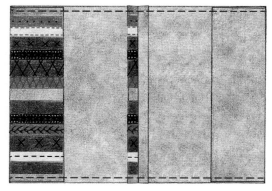

diag 9

Reposition the long yellow ribbon across the whole width of the cover and glue in place as before. Work even cross stitches along the centre of the ribbon.

Slip the front and back edge of the book into the flaps to cover the book. Tie a bow on the yellow ribbon.

stitches and
techniques

stitches

attaching a bead

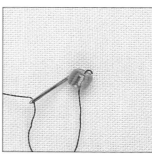

1. Secure the thread on the back of the fabric and bring it to the front. Thread the bead onto the needle.

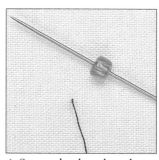

2. Slide the bead down the thread to the fabric. Take the needle to the back at the end of the bead.

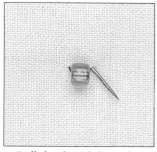

3. Pull the thread through. Re-emerge at the other end of the bead.

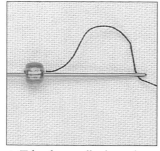

4. Take the needle through the bead again.

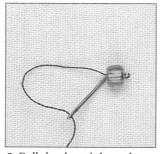

5. Pull the thread through. Take needle to back of the fabric at the end of the bead.

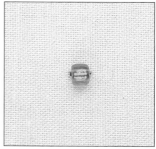

6. Pull the thread through. End off on the back of the fabric.

back stitch Back stitch is a line stitch and is well suited to follow tight curves. Work the stitches from right to left.

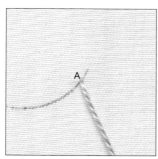

1. Bring the thread to the front at A, a stitch length from the right hand end of the marked line.

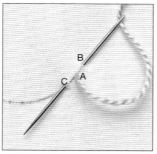

2. Take the needle to the back at B, at the beginning of the marked line. Emerge at C. The distance from A to C should be the same as the distance from A to B.

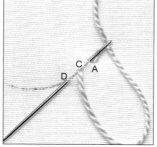

3. Pull thread through to complete the first stitch. Take the needle to the back at A, through the same hole in the fabric. Emerge at D.

4. Continue working stitches in this way, keeping them even. To finish, take the needle to the back and end off.

blanket stitch

Traditionally used for edging blankets and rugs, blanket stitch can be worked as a surface embroidery stitch as well as an edging stitch and is commonly used for appliqué. Work the stitches from left to right.

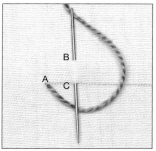

1. Bring the thread to the front at A. Take the needle from B to C. Make sure the thread is under the tip of the needle.

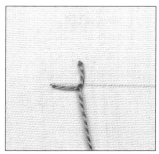

2. Pull the thread towards you until the loop rests gently against the emerging thread.

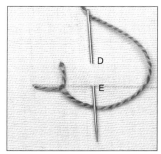

3. Take the needle from D to E, a short distance from the previous stitch. Make sure the thread is under the tip of the needle.

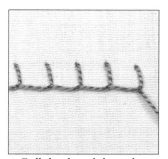

4. Pull the thread through as before. Continue working stitches in this way.

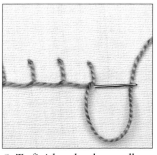

5. To finish, take the needle to the back of the fabric just over the last loop and secure.

blanket stitch pinwheel

Often called blanket pinwheels, these are formed from blanket stitches worked in a circle radiating from the centre.

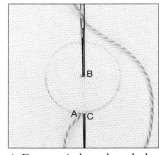

1. Draw a circle and mark the centre. Bring the thread to front at A. Take the needle from the centre B to C.

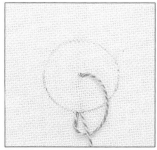

2. Place the thread under the needle tip. Begin to pull the thread through, pulling away from the circle.

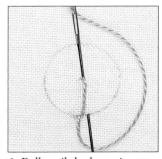

3. Pull until the loop sits on the circle. Take the needle from the centre to the edge. Ensure the thread is under the needle.

4. Continue working stitches around the circle, rotating the fabric as you work.

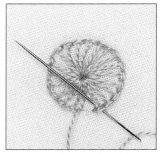

5. For the last stitch, slide the needle under the first stitch without catching the fabric.

6. Pull the thread through. Take the needle through the centre to complete the pinwheel.

chain stitch

This very versatile stitch can be used as an outline or in close rows as a filling stitch. Take care not to pull the loops too tight as they will lose their rounded shape. The stitch is worked from the top towards you.

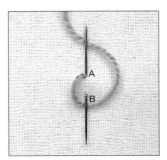

1. Bring the thread to the front at A. Take the needle from A to B, using the same hole in the fabric at A. Loop the thread under the tip of the needle.

2. Pull the thread through until the loop lies snugly around the emerging thread.

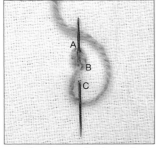

3. Take the needle through the same hole in the fabric at B and emerge at C. Ensure the thread is under the tip of the needle.

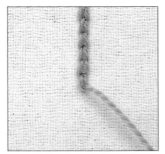

4. Pull the thread through as before. Continue working stitches in the same manner for the required distance.

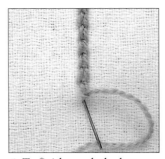

5. To finish, work the last stitch and take the needle to the back of the fabric just over the loop.

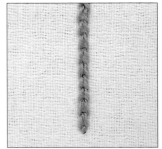

6. Pull the thread through to form a short straight stitch. End off the thread on the back of the fabric.

cross stitch

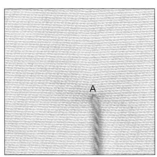

1. Bring the thread to the front at A, in the lower right hand corner of the stitch.

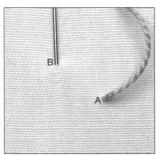

2. Take the needle to the back at B, in the upper left hand corner of the stitch.

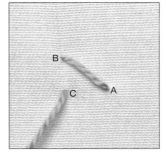

3. Pull the thread through to form the first diagonal stitch. Emerge at C, in the lower left hand corner of the stitch.

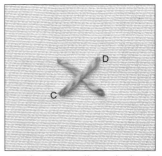

4. Take the needle to the back at D, diagonally opposite. Pull the thread through and secure on the back.

detached chain

This is also commonly known as lazy daisy. Detached chain is a looped stitch, which can be worked alone or in groups and is often used to create leaves and flowers with each petal being a single detached chain.

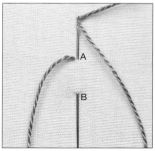

1. Bring the needle to the front at the top of the stitch at A. Take the needle to the back as close as possible to A and emerge at B.

2. Loop the thread under the tip of the needle.

3. Keeping your left thumb over the loop, pull the thread through. The tighter you pull, the thinner the stitch will become.

4. To anchor the stitch, take the thread to the back just over the loop.

feather stitch

Feather stitch is a delicate stitch, often used to decorate baby and children's clothing. The stitch can vary greatly in appearance, depending on the angle of the needle and the length of the stitches. The tension, needle angle and stitch length must be kept consistent throughout to ensure even stitches.

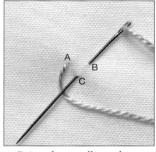

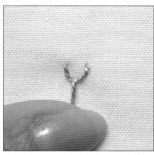

1. Bring the needle to the front at A. Loop the thread to the right and take the needle from B to C. The loop is under the needle.

2. Pull the thread through in a downward movement, holding the thread firmly with your thumb.

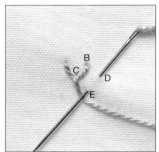

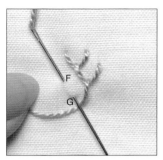

3. Take the needle from D to E. E is directly below B. Loop the thread under the needle tip.

4. Pull the thread through.

5. Take the needle from F to G. Loop the thread under the needle and hold in place.

6. Continue, following steps 3 - 5. Finish with a tiny stitch over the last loop.

french knot

The traditional French knot was worked with one wrap around the needle, however today it is often worked with more. To create a larger knot, it is neater to use a thicker thread rather than making too many wraps.

1. Bring the thread to the front. Hold the thread firmly with your thumb and index finger 3cm (1¼") away from the fabric.

2. Bring the thread over the needle. Ensure the needle points away from the fabric.

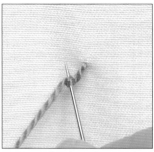

3. Wrap the thread around the needle. Keeping the thread taut, begin to turn the point of the needle towards the fabric.

4. Take the needle to the back 1 - 2 fabric threads away from where it emerged.

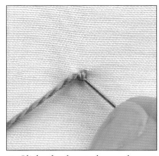

5. Slide the knot down the needle onto the fabric. Pull the thread until the knot sits firmly around the needle.

6. Hold the wrap in place with your thumb. Push the needle through the wrap. Pull from the back until a firm knot forms on the fabric.

herringbone stitch Also known as plaited stitch and catch stitch, it is often used to work decorative borders.

Stitch between two parallel lines marked with magic tape. Space the stitches closer or wider apart for the desired effect.

1. Bring the thread to the front at A. With the thread below the needle, take a small stitch from right to left on the upper line, to the right of A.

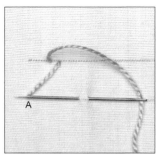

2. Pull the thread through. With the thread above the needle take a small stitch from right to left on the lower line, to the right of A.

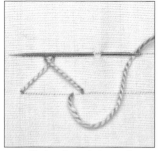

3. Pull the thread through. With the thread below the needle, take a small stitch on the upper line, the same distance away as before.

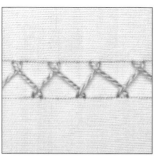

4. Continue working evenly spaced stitches, alternating between the lower and upper lines.

row of sequins

This is a quick and easy method of attaching rows of sequins, keeping the stitching almost invisible. Each sequin is attached with a back stitch through the centre hole.

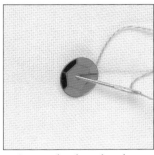

1. Secure the thread and bring it to the front half a sequin's width from the end of the line. Place a sequin at the end of the line and take the needle through the centre.

2. Bring the thread to the front half a sequin's width from the first.

3. Place a second sequin, overlapping half of the first. Take the needle to the back through the hole at the edge of the first sequin.

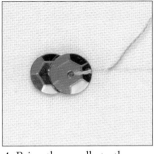

4. Bring the needle to the front ahead of the second sequin.

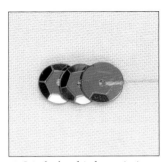

5. Stitch the third sequin in place with a back stitch in the same way.

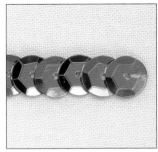

6. Continue to the end of the row.

running stitch
This is one of the quickest and easiest stitches of all but it will not cover a marked line.

Make the stitches uniform in length and slightly longer on the front than on the back. Running stitch is worked from right to left.

1. Bring the thread to the front on the right hand end of the line to be stitched.

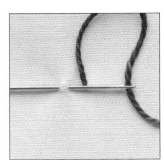

2. Take a small stitch, skimming the needle beneath the fabric along the line.

3. Pull the thread through. Take another stitch as before, ensuring the stitch is the same length as the previous stitch.

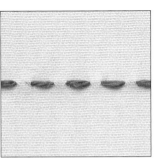

4. Continue in the same manner to the end of the line.

stem stitch

This very versatile stitch is ideal for fine lines and curves. It can also be used as a filling stitch when worked in close rows. Work stem stitch from left to right, keeping the thread below the needle.

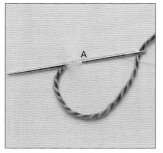

1. Bring the needle to the front at the left hand end of the line. With the thread below the needle, take it to the back at A. Re-emerge at the end of the line.

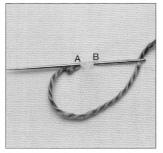

2. Pull the thread through. Again with the thread below the needle, take the needle from B to A.

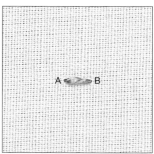

3. Pull the thread through. Continue working the stitches in the same way, always keeping the thread below the needle and the stitches the same size.

4. To end off, take the needle to the back for the last stitch but do not re-emerge. Secure the thread on the back.

straight stitch

This is the most basic embroidery stitch of all. It can be worked in any direction and to any length.

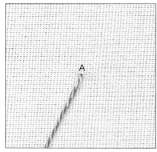

1. Bring the thread to the front at the beginning of the stitch, A.

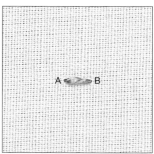

2. Take the needle to the back at the end of the stitch, B.

3. Pull the thread through. Work a second stitch in the same manner.

4. Straight stitches worked at different angles.

techniques

appliqué

Appliqué is a fun and easy way to attach a design to a base fabric. The edges of the appliqué pieces are usually edged with blanket stitch for a neat finish (see page 73). The templates for fused appliqué are mirrored in order for the finished design to face in the right direction. When using appliqué paper protect your iron and ironing board with a cloth. We used contrasting thread for photographic purposes.

 HINT If you are using felt for your appliqué make sure to use wool felt as acrylic felt can melt under the iron.

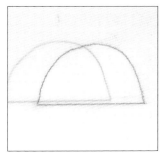

1. Trace the templates onto the smooth side of the appliqué paper.

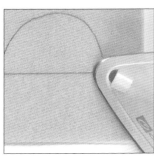

2. Place the appliqué paper, with the smooth side facing up, over the wrong side of the fabric piece.

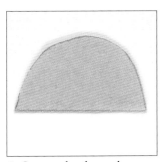

3. Cut out the shape along the traced lines.

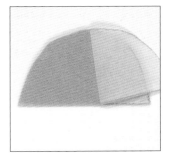

4. Peel away the backing paper.

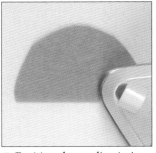

5. Position the appliqué piece onto the main fabric with the right side of the fabric facing up. Fuse the piece in place with a warm, dry iron.

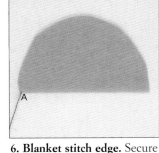

6. Blanket stitch edge. Secure the thread on the back. Bring the thread to the front at A, just outside the edge of the appliqué piece.

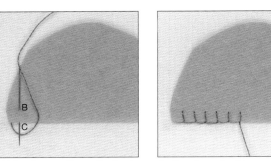

7. Take the needle to the back at B, through the appliqué piece. Emerge at C, just outside the edge. Keep the thread under the tip of the needle.

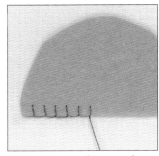

8. Continue in this way along the edge of the appliqué piece, keeping the stitches even.

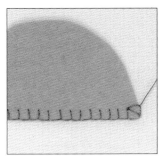

9. Turning a corner. Work three blanket stitches into the same hole to turn a corner or point.

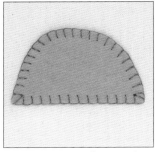

10. Continue stitching in this way to outline the shape.

attaching buttons

Whether you are using buttons as decoration or as a fastener, it is important that they are stitched in place securely. You can use a matching thread if you don't want it to show or a contrasting thread for decorative purposes.

1. Knot the end of a doubled thread. Secure the thread on the wrong side at the position for the button.

2. Bring the thread to the front and through one hole in the button. Centre the button over the stitch (diag 1).

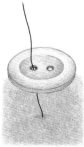

diag 1   *diag 2*

3. Take the needle down through the second hole and through the fabric close to where the thread emerged (diag 2).

4. Work another 3 - 4 stitches into the pair of holes, taking the needle through the same holes in the fabric (diag 3).

diag 3

5. End off securely on the back by taking the needle through the stitches on the back several times (diag 4).

diag 4

6. Buttons with four holes can be stitched in place with two parallel stitches or with a cross stitch.

fringing All woven fabrics can be fringed along the edges.

1. Trim the fabric to the finished size, cutting along the grain of the fabric (diag 1).

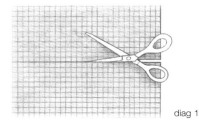

diag 1

2. Use a needle to ease out the fabric threads one at a time along each side to make the fringe (diag 2).

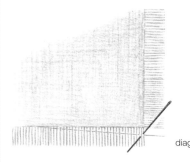

diag 2

gathering

To gather up long pieces of fabric, such as the tutu on page 34, it is easiest to use a sewing machine. However smaller pieces are just as easy to do by hand.

1. Use a machine sewing thread and tie a knot on the end. Secure the thread at one side of the edge you wish to gather.

2. Weave the needle up and down along the edge of the fabric, taking it through only a small amount of fabric for each stitch (diag 1).

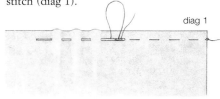

diag 1

3. When you reach the opposite side, pull the thread gently to gather up the fabric (diag 2). Continue to pull until the gathered edge is the required length. Secure the thread.

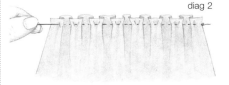

diag 2

gathered flowers
Simple but effective flowers can be made from ribbons or strips of fabric using this method. We used contrasting thread for photographic purposes.

1. Cut a length of ribbon or fabric.

2. Knot the end of a matching sewing thread. Fold one end of the ribbon to the back and take the needle through the fold to the front.

3. Work small even gathering stitches along one side of the ribbon.

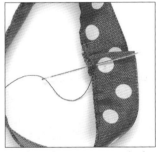

4. Place the opposite end of ribbon behind the folded end and take the needle to the front through all layers.

5. Pull the thread firmly to gather the ribbon tightly at the centre.

6. Secure the gathers with two or three tiny stitches at the centre. Leave the thread tail on the back to secure later.

plaiting

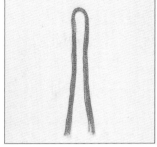

1. Fold the thread bundle in half to find the centre.

2. Secure the folded end temporarily.

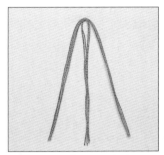

3. Separate the strands into three equal groups.

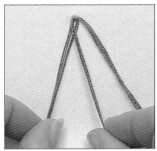

4. Take the left hand group of threads over the middle group. The left hand group now becomes the middle group.

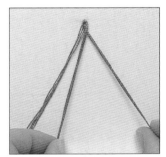

5. Take the right hand group of threads over the middle group. The right hand group now becomes the middle group.

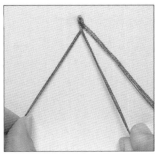

6. Take the left hand group of threads over the middle group.

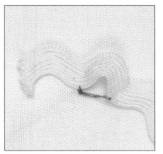

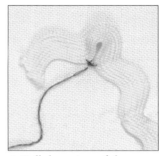

7. Continue in this manner, alternating from side to side until reaching the end of the threads.

8. Knot the threads to secure the plait.

5. Take the needle to the back at the centre and begin to pull the thread through.

6. Pull the points of the ricrac together to form the first petal.

ricrac flower

The waves in the ricrac braid are pulled together to form the petals of these decorative little flowers.

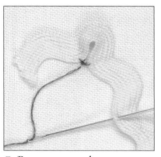

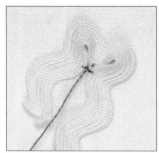

7. Re-emerge at the centre. Take the needle through the third inside point of the ricrac.

8. Take the thread to the back at the centre and pull the stitch taut, pulling the points together to form the second petal.

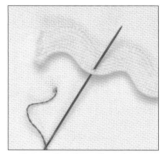

1. Cut a length of ricrac so there are seven full curves on one side.

2. Bring the thread to the front through the fabric at the marked flower centre. Take the needle through the first point on the inside edge of the ricrac.

9. Stitch another two points of the ricrac in the same way to form petals three and four.

10. Stitch into the next inside point of the ricrac. Trim the ricrac a short distance from the point.

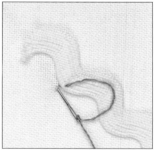

3. Take the needle back through the marked centre.

4. Bring the thread to the front just next to the first stitch and through the second inside point of the ricrac.

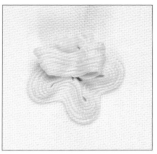

11. Fold the raw edge to the back and pull the stitch taut, placing the fold over the starting point.

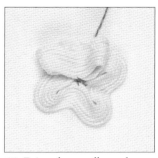

12. Bring the needle to the front at the outer edge of the ricrac between petals one and five.

13. Take the needle through all layers at the outer edge to secure the fold.

14. Finishing. Bring the needle to the front inside the fold in the fifth petal, through the raw ends of the ricrac underneath.

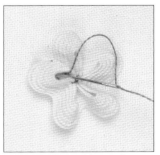

15. Take the needle to the back at the same point to catch the ends in place under the petal.

suffolk puffs
Suffolk puffs are made from a circle of fabric that is hand gathered around the outer edge. The longer the running stitches used for the gathering, the smaller the opening at the centre will be. Using tiny running stitches will result in a larger opening at the centre.

1. Using a circular template of the required size, cut out a circle of fabric. Thread a needle with matching machine sewing thread.

2. With wrong sides together, fold under 3mm (1/8") around the entire edge of the circle and finger press.

3. Beginning on the wrong side and using running stitches, stitch along the folded edge.

4. Firmly pull up the running stitches to gather the fabric.

5. Secure the thread with 2 - 3 tiny back stitches. Take the thread inside the puff and re-emerge a short distance away.

6. Flatten the puff, keeping the gathering at the centre. Gently pull the thread and snip it close to the fabric.

patterns

Some of the patterns and designs on the following pages will need to be enlarged using a photocopier to acheive the correct size.

Follow the instructions for each pattern and design using the ratio.

poppy

page 54
pattern and design

 ricrac flower

O   gathered flower

+   looped ribbon flower

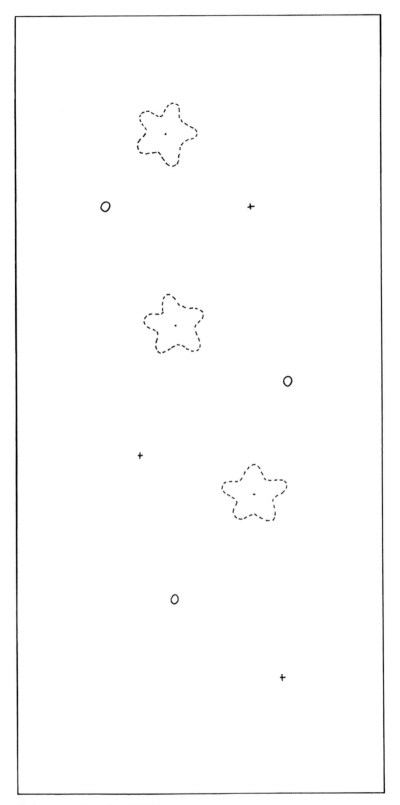

Enlarge pattern by 125%

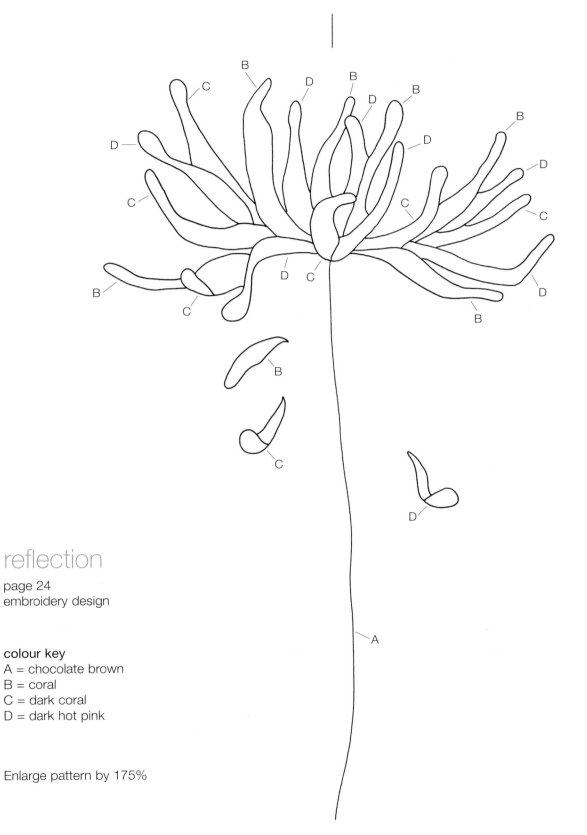

reflection

page 24
embroidery design

colour key
A = chocolate brown
B = coral
C = dark coral
D = dark hot pink

Enlarge pattern by 175%

happy feet

page 28
pattern and templates

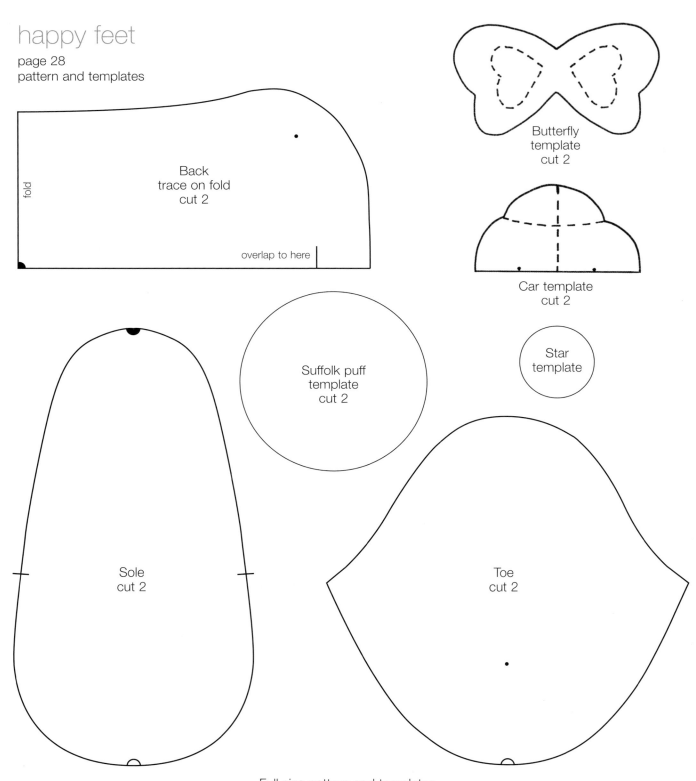

Back
trace on fold
cut 2

overlap to here

fold

Butterfly
template
cut 2

Car template
cut 2

Star
template

Suffolk puff
template
cut 2

Sole
cut 2

Toe
cut 2

Full size pattern and templates

spring

page 38
embroidery design

Full size pattern

centre

align with upper raw edge

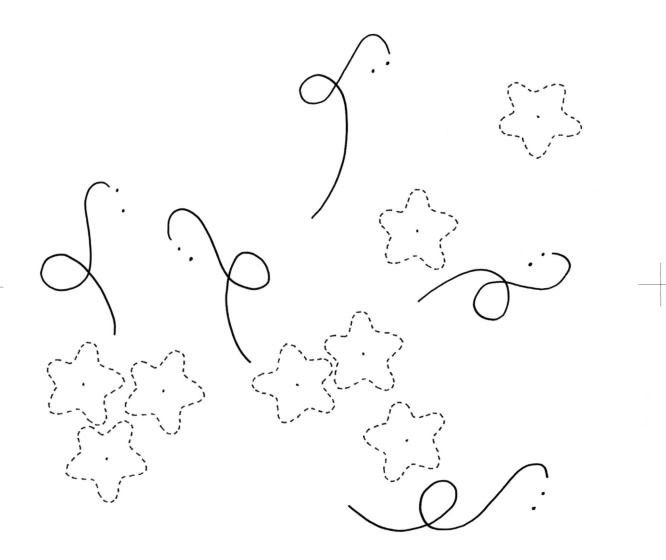

impressions

page 44
embroidery design

Enlarge design by 200%

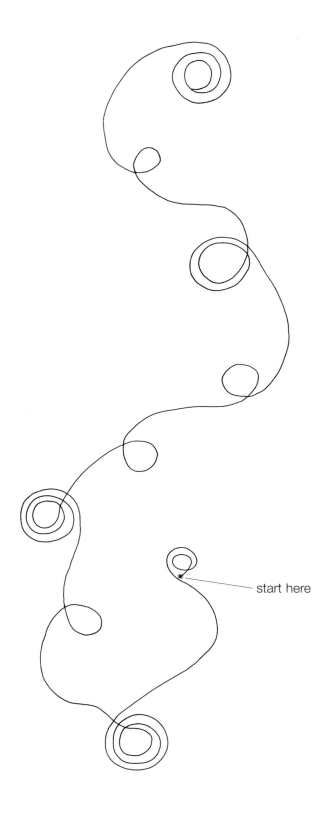

start here

first prize

page 50
design and template

Enlarge design by 120%

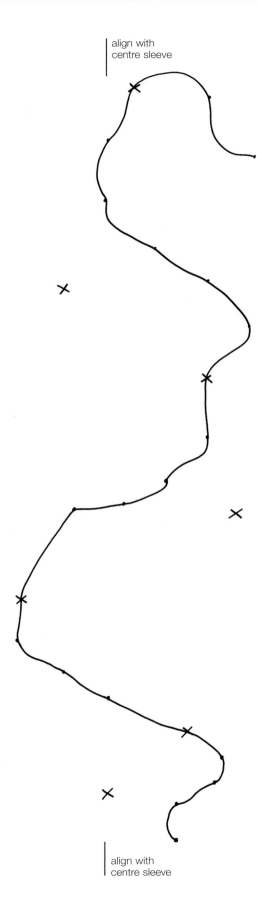

align with
centre sleeve

align with
centre sleeve

Felt template
Full size
cut 4 red felt
cut 5 white felt

garnish

page 58
embroidery design

Apron
Enlarge design by 170%

Oven mitt
Full size

snug as a bug

page 64
appliqué templates

Enlarge patterns
by 135%

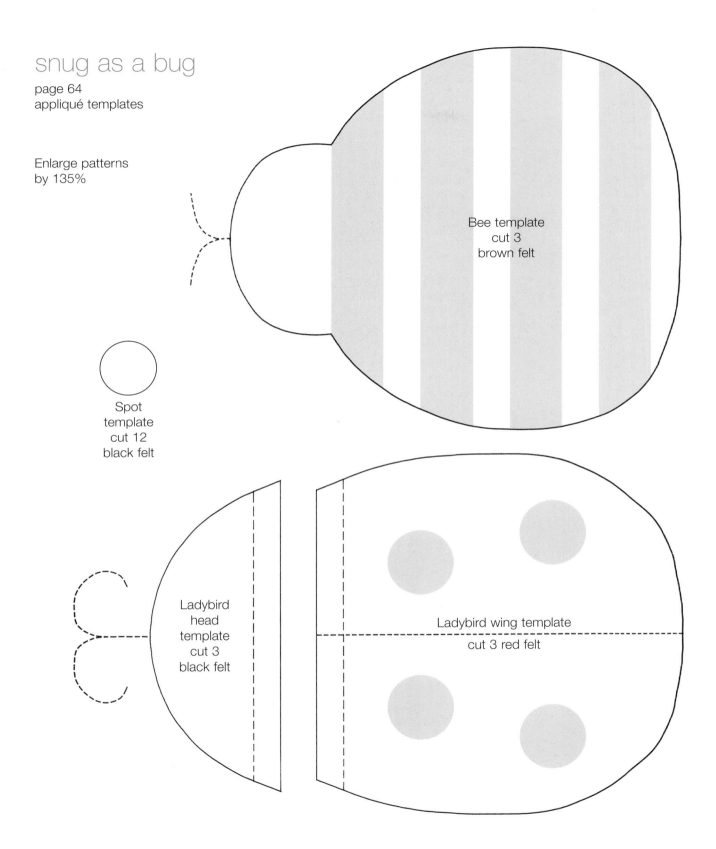

Bee template
cut 3
brown felt

Spot
template
cut 12
black felt

Ladybird
head
template
cut 3
black felt

Ladybird wing template

cut 3 red felt

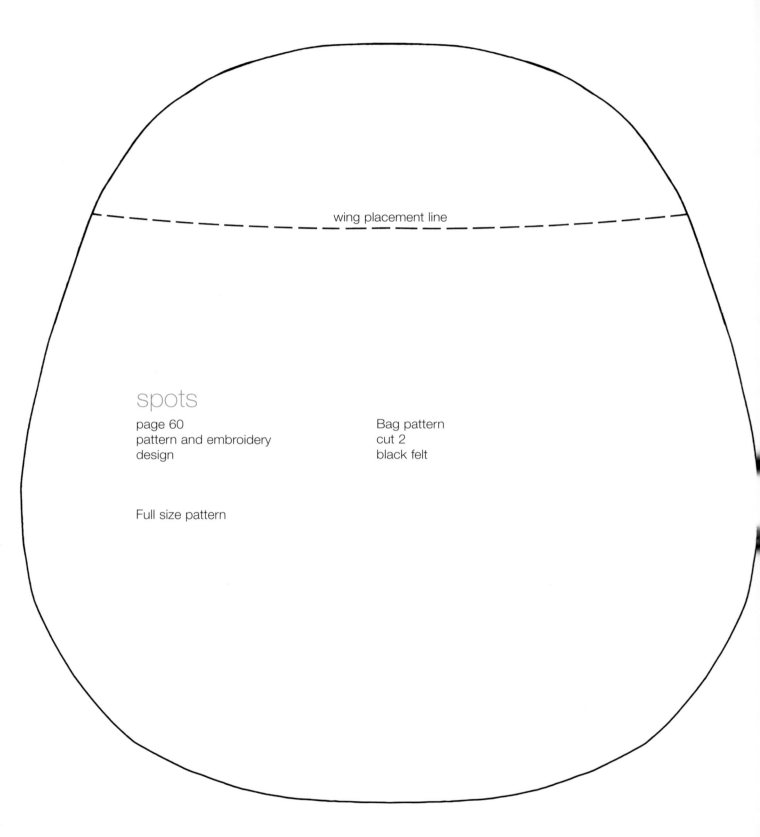

wing placement line

spots

page 60
pattern and embroidery
design

Bag pattern
cut 2
black felt

Full size pattern

spots

page 60
pattern and embroidery design

Full size pattern

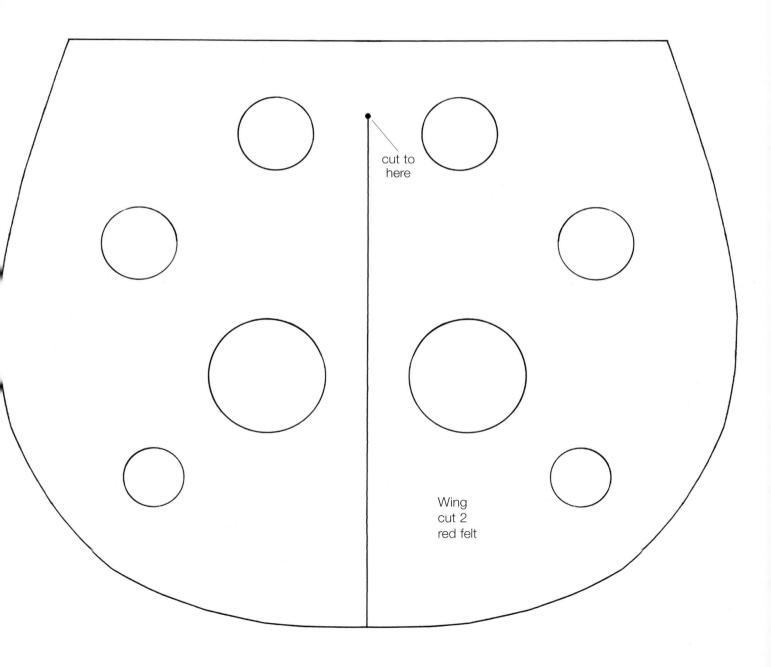

cut to
here

Wing
cut 2
red felt

index